TIGERS
in the DARK

TIGERS
in the DARK

THOMAS LANE BUTTS

HB Publications
Mobile

TIGERS IN THE DARK

ISBN 0-940882-19-1
(previously ISBN 0-687-42080-6)

Cover design by Melissa M. Bowden
for Tom Mason Communications.

Scripture quotations are from the Revised Standard Ver-
sion Common Bible, copyrighted © 1973.

Scripture quotations noted Phillips are from the New
Testament in Modern English, copyright © J.B. Phillips
1958, 1960, 1972.

Manufactured by Walsworth Publishing Company,
Marceline, Missouri, United States of America.

HB Publications
P.O. Box 2806
Mobile, Alabama 36652

To
Hilda, Lane, Becca,
Whose Daily Love Sustains Me

Contents

Foreword

Is it possible to have a religious faith with a practical use for everyday living? Can a Christian whose religion dates back to the first century find Christianity significant in the technological twentieth century? Can the person with a religious faith find meaningful living, surrounded by high-speed machinery, computerization, rapid cultural changes, space exploration, and instantaneous mass communications?

These questions are pertinent queries for the contemporary person who confronts the swirl of daily life with its ups and downs, constant decisions, and continuous mobility. As we rapidly approach the year A.D. 2000, our culture is not only fast-moving, constantly changing, and rather restless, it also requires a life-style with a means for continuous stability and life adjustment. One of the results of living in the contemporary culture is a general psychic depression that affects our moods. There is more confusion today than in past eras because there are more decisions to be made about everything, more alternatives in everything ranging from where to work, finding a gratifying career, where to live, and living through generation gaps. There is a decline in the former close and direct relationships between employers and employees, along with a lessening of vocational gratification as persons have to deal with assembly lines, machines, computers, and impersonal mass numbers. The modern world is polycentric and pluralistic, and individuals must manage to cope or they cannot survive, much less be well-adjusted. The quest of the twentieth-century pilgrim requires finding a meaningful relationship between the Christian faith and vast, impersonal systems, implacable bureaucracies, and the depersonalizing dimensions of contemporary society.

According to Tom Butts, there *are* some answers and solutions to the dilemmas of Christian living for twentieth-century persons who long for personal identity and secure roots in the earth that God created. Tom sees some suggestions and solutions within the personhood of the individual relating to a pressure-filled and frustrating world. With low-key and dynamically oriented compassion, he sees a real connection between Christian faith, meaningful living, and the search for authentic personhood. Looking at life through his own theologized spectacles, he has a vision about living and has tested that vision in the crucible of real life situations. With a wide variety of experiences in his own living, observing, and ministering, he has discovered for himself the legitimate connection between the Christian faith and authentic selfhood. Tom Butts is a consummate pastor and a wise parish theologian.

Not a man of unrealistic idealism or a "preacher turned psychologist" with Bible words and armchair analysis, Tom is a deeply sensitive person who has successfully synthesized the sometimes abstract and complex concepts of theology, integrating them into his daily living. Thus he serves others through hard-earned insights. Taking a cue from the noted psychologist Abraham Maslow, who felt that normal and healthy persons are proper subjects for study, Tom faces human happiness and human suffering with equal facility. In his theology, he has achieved a successful balance of biblical wholeness and individual human growth. He is sympathetic with the gruesome struggles of psychic pain, thus his ministry is oriented toward persons who are in need and those who are in the process of growing emotionally. As a result, his friends and parishoners are richer because of his supportive love.

One of the major needs of any mature person is honesty. A person cannot be a healthy Christian without openly facing the Lord in order to face others in honesty. How do we get to that level of selfhood? How do we mature and at the same time be intellectually honest and authentic Christian persons? Or, to put it theologically, how do we grow in grace? Unless we are able to master the ability to mature, Christianity becomes the empty exercise of a social gesture on Sunday morning in church and has nothing to do with real living. Tom Butts understands that to reach Christian maturity requires effort. He knows that emotional growth is painful, but it is necessary for a wholesome enjoyment of life as one becomes liberated by the gospel.

With our feet of fragile clay, many of us hamper emotional growth through various forms of neurotic fretting that are basically unchristian. All of us tend to fall into a pattern of fighting unseen enemies. But real living comes from openness, healthy relationships with other persons, and avoiding the obviously impossible standards we frequently impose on ourselves. Tom's writing, living, and thinking reflect the delicate art of balanced living. In this book, he shares his experiences openly and invites the reader to reflect and examine. He has developed the knack of blending the blessings of the gospel with the daily dirt under our feet.

Having known Tom as a person, pastor, and friend, I can tell you that he is a man of instant engagement who makes a stranger feel he is with a friend of long standing. In his travels he meets many fellow pilgrims and holds up a guiding light for them so they can see the way. As pilgrims together, they move through the flickering shadows of life in the constant quest for a deeper and more personal experience with God.

I wish there were more preachers like him.

David Abernathy
Producer
THE PROTESTANT HOUR

Preface

The seed thoughts in this book can be traced back to my own personal struggles more than twenty-five years ago. Any insights found in these pages are but the reflected light of creative encounters with numerous persons along the way during that time. Two loving parents and four brothers and sisters whose love nourished my early life constitute the foundation of old that has made life stable enough to look for answers.

The Reverend Edward P. Dixon, erstwhile chaplain at Cook County Hospital in Chicago, has had a profound influence on my life and ministry. During six months of clinical pastoral education under his supervision, I found the motivation and power to struggle creatively with my own "tigers in the dark." To some persons, I owe a debt of appreciation, but to Chaplain Dixon, I owe my life.

One of the greatest sources of strength, courage, and insight has been my involvement with persons who were living through a crisis experience. It is from these creative encounters that this book has been written. The opportunity of walking into the inner sanctum of other human lives is one of the most unique privileges afforded a minister. From this privilege, I have learned most of what I know.

I am indebted to the Joint Communications Committee of The United Methodist Church for the invitation to preach on the 1978 United Methodist Series of "The Protestant Hour," which gave me occasion to write, in thematic form, the material of which this book consists. Most of all, I am indebted to David Abernathy, executive director and producer of "The Protestant Hour," for his incisive editorial help and, not least of all, his encouragement.

I am grateful to two faithful church secretaries, Willenne Finn and Anne Stults, who worked untiringly to type this manuscript more times than any of us care to remember.

TLB

Fighting Tigers
in the Dark

Ephesians 6:10-20

Several years ago there was a well-known television circus show that developed a Bengal tiger act. Like the rest of the show, it was done "live" before a large audience. One evening, the tiger trainer went into the cage with several tigers to do a routine performance. The door was locked behind him. The spotlights highlighted the cage, the television cameras moved in close, and the audience watched in suspense as the trainer skillfully put the tigers through their paces. In the middle of the performance the worst possible fate befell the act: the lights went out! For twenty or thirty long, dark seconds the trainer was locked in with the tigers. In the darkness they could see him, but he could not see them. A whip and a small kitchen chair seemed meager protection under the circumstances, but he survived and when the lights came on calmly finished the performance. In an interview afterward, he was asked how he felt knowing that the tigers could see him but that he could not see them. He first admitted the chilling fear of the situation, but pointed out that the tigers *did not know* that he could not see them. He said, "I just kept cracking my whip and talking to them until the lights came on. And they never knew that I could not see them as well as they could see me.''

This experience gives us a vivid parable of human life. At some point in our lives, all of us face the terrifying task of fighting tigers in the dark. Some face it constantly. Many people cope daily with internal problems that are capable of destroying them. They cannot visualize their problems or understand them, but their problems seem to have them zeroed in. They struggle unproductively with unseen enemies nibbling away at them from every side. These people are not concerned with how to get a "tiger in their tank," but with how to handle the untamed creatures of the night with which they are already forced to cope.

No one could hope to catalog the whole expanse of unseen enemies that constitute every person's dark world of the subconscious. There are innumerable demonic forces that rise up from the unfathomed depths to mystify, frighten, and immobilize. Because some of these forces and feelings are unique to the personality in which they occur, there is the additional concern that individually we seem to have problems that no one else has. But some of these tigers in the dark are so common that all of us are familiar with their unseen roar.

For example, we are besieged by unexplained hostility that slips in on us at the most inappropriate times and for the most inexplicable reasons. Such feelings are born of unresolved resentments and negative feelings that were denied and pushed into the subconscious mind. This tiger, which once could have been fought in the light, returns with multiplied advantages to claw us in the darkness of the night. Until the hostility is traced back to its origin and resolved, the struggle to handle it will continue to be a terrifying and unproductive battle with an unseen enemy in the dark.

Another tiger, often created by hostility and many other forces, is guilt. This is a treacherous and evasive enemy! How often we see his victims, wounded and bleeding, trying to shake him off their sore backs! Guilt is a normal by-product of daily living. It can be handled in a healthy fashion as long as there is a conscious connection between some realistic wrong and the feeling of guilt. But when the reason for feeling guilty becomes obscured, guilt becomes a tiger in the dark. Have you ever felt a deep sense of being wrong, without knowing why? Have you ever felt a deep sense of guilt about a trivial matter that you intellectually knew should not cause guilt at all? Have you ever been shocked by the conspicuous absence of guilt about something that should have made you feel guilty? The tiger of guilt, invisible though he may be, can confuse your relationships with people, destroy your relationship with God, and bleed life of the last drop of joy. Some people are walking bundles of guilt, but they don't know why. They are compulsively religious, forever evangelizing, and always confessing. But they never experience relief because they don't know why they feel guilty. This tiger remains invisible until the vital connection between the feeling and the cause can be established.

Both the tigers of hostility and guilt produce yet another deadly animal of the night—depression. Wherever you find hostility and guilt, you may be sure that depression is lurking somewhere nearby. Depression is a familiar tiger to us all. When it latches its claws into our backs, at best we are miserable and at worst we are in great danger. It is a pervading spiritual loneliness, which in its mildest form gives us the mulligrubs and at its worst drags us into a "dark night of the soul." There is always a reason when we are depressed, and relief may not come by knowing the reason. But you may be sure that relief will not come until we do know. Always, the difference between a fair fight in the light and a fearful bout in the dark is to have a connection between what we feel and why we feel it. Remove that connection and what was once a tame pussycat in the light becomes a tiger in the dark.

These three tigers—guilt, hostility, and depression—must have been part of what the apostle Paul meant when he warned us that we fight not against flesh and blood, or against a visible enemy, but against enemies that are unseen. "We are up against the unseen power that controls this dark world, and spiritual agents from the very headquarters of evil" (Phillips). Fighting tigers in the dark is not a sport of recent invention. Paul knew about it from personal experience. He knew the accompanying terrors, and he suggests in Ephesians that we appropriately arm ourselves for this nocturnal battle.

Most of us would be surprised, if not shocked, to know what is going on in the lives of the people with whom we brush elbows each day. If you but knew the inner struggle and mounting fears, the personal tragedy and the constant conflict, the gnawing feelings of inadequacy and the suppressed thoughts and urges, which lurk in the dark recesses of the lives of people around you, you would be appalled. Occasionally we inadvertently glimpse some aspect (or symptom) of this private tiger act in the behavior of some person near us. But, like the visible tip of an iceberg, what we see does not reveal nearly all there is of it.

FIGHTING TIGERS IN THE DARK

We tend to be critical of people whose feelings and behavior are strange, but our criticism is usually born of ignorance of the unseen reasons for such feelings and behavior. If we only knew the fearful tigers they battle daily, we would rush to their sides to aid them rather than stand back and criticize. Have you ever caught a big fish and had him give you a real fight before you landed him? It was fun. But have you ever wondered what the other fish down there thought when they saw their old friend suddenly go wild and start flagellating? They don't see the hook or line, or realize that he is caught, and his behavior seems inexplicably strange. If they had known that he was hooked and hurting, they could have better understood why he acted so unlike himself. Most odd and antisocial behavior is born of frustrating internal battles, which many of us are not sensitive enough to perceive or compassionate enough to understand. The boisterous bully whose conduct and attitudes is repulsive is very likely an insecure person trying to compensate for his feelings of inadequacy. If you fight with him or scorn him, you will deepen his problem and confirm his fear of inadequacy. But if you treat him with love and respect, you will open the door to understanding and help. While your efforts to love and understand may not be strong enough to break him from his antisocial ways, at least you will make sure that his ways do not become your ways. The people you know who are hard to live with are in fact having a struggle living with themselves. Behind the facade of pretension they are likely battling for their lives with unseen tigers of the night. You can return hostility for hostility. But in the process, you become a part of the problem and thus allow other people's problems to become yours. One alternative is to be mature enough to use love and understanding as a means of resolving their problem.

In his book *Guilt and Grace,* Paul Tournier describes the general harmfulness of unsolicited criticism and the spirit of judgment we find so easy to exercise toward people. At one point Dr. Tournier says categorically, "All criticism is destructive." It is easy for us to fall into the widespread illusion that we can help people by denouncing their faults, without even being invited to do so. This is an illusion all too commonly practiced in the good name of Jesus. Any time you hear someone say, "I don't want to criticize, but—" you may be sure that everything following that disarming introduction makes a lie of it.[1]

Most of us are ill-equipped to tell someone else what to do because of the imperfection of our own knowledge. We always err dangerously in offering unsolicited advice. All around us are masses of wounded, distressed, and crushed people whose daily struggle with life is a more serious battle than we would ever dream.

When we think about how we may help others in their struggle, the key is understanding and love. When we think about how we may manage our own fight with tigers in the dark, we would do well to remember what the tiger trainer said he did while the lights were out. He said, "I just kept cracking my whip and talking to them until the lights came on." If we must fight with unseen enemies (and some day, some way, we will), then we need to prepare to practice that courageous art of continuing to crack our whip while waiting for the light.

---

[1] Paul Tournier, *Guilt and Grace* (New York: Harper, 1962), pp. 80-81.

FIGHTING TIGERS IN THE DARK

Several years ago my two small children were playing in the backyard after dark. Suddenly we heard them scream with fear, and before we could get to them they came tumbling over each other through the back door. Breathless and white with fear, they told me that there was a huge animal with big teeth in the backyard. They said it looked like a tiger. I got what weapons I could find, called a neighbor, and we took a powerful light and went to look for this creature. We found the animal crouching in the corner of the backyard. We called the children to come and see him in the light. It was only a half-grown, stray Persian cat, which later became a family pet. But in the darkness, he looked like a tiger to the children. In the light, he was merely a playful and harmless kitten. The light of clearer understanding from our heavenly Father will make harmless kittens of many of the fears we once thought were tigers in the dark.

The Longing for Belonging

Luke 9:23-25

All of us are born with the need to belong. That need is culturally written into our blood. There is no age or stage of life when we are free from this need. We see this need to belong all the way from the infant who clings to his mother to the lonely truckdriver who tries to find a temporary "electronic belonging" on his CB radio.

In his book *The Identity Society,* William Glasser says that "the need for involvement has been built into our nervous systems for the last half-million years. We always need involvement, and we always feel pain when we have none. The pain warns us to seek involvement with others."

If we fail to achieve involvement with others, there is always one possibility left: self-involvement. As unsatisfactory as this is in comparison with involvement with others, self-involvement will reduce and sometimes temporarily eliminate the pain of being alone. But because we need involvement with others, self-involvement is an inadequate alternative. We cannot fool our nervous system for long. We quickly become dissatisfied with self-involvement, and the pain of our emptiness and nonbelonging returns.[1]

Alienation and estrangement are unnatural conditions for humankind. Personal identity and purpose for life are part of the fact and feeling of belonging. I refer to fact and feeling because no matter how much or to what we belong, unless we have a *feeling* of belonging, we do not actually belong. All of us know people, in fact we may *be* people, who belong to every club in town and who attend a half-dozen committee meetings each week but who are still lonely and alienated. These persons are frantically searching for what it seems they should in fact already have. You can belong and still fail to have a *sense* of belonging.

One of the deepest tragedies of life is that there are so many people who feel unwanted, unneeded, unloved, and unappreciated. People do many unhappy and harmful things to themselves and to others because of loneliness, alienation, and a sense of nonbelonging. Those who do not feel that they belong often compensate by trying to possess both people and things, both of which are spiritually dangerous and virtually counterproductive. The good life does not consist of the abundance of *things* or *persons* that we own. There is hardly a way you can ever experience a warm and satisfying sense of belonging to something or someone that you own. Our deepest and greatest need is not to possess but to be "possessed." In the final analysis, our stature is not measured by what belongs to us, but by that to which we belong. As Jesus put it, "For what does it profit a person if he gain the whole world, and yet loses himself."

---

[1] William Glasser, *The Identity Society* (New York: Harper, 1972), pp. 74-75.

A number of years ago Dianna Barrymore wrote an autobiography entitled *Too Much Too Soon*. After I read this catalog of human tragedy, I felt that the book should have been entitled "Too Little Too Late." This tragic autobiography is a classic example of the kind of emotional and spiritual decay that takes place when there is no sense of belonging. Early in the book the author gives the key to her unhappy life when she says, "I didn't have love. I never belonged."

There is much pain in the lives of people who don't feel they have been accepted by persons whose acceptance is important. Each of us may hold the key to some kingdom or realm where we have the power to say to some "enter" and to others "go; we want no part of you." Likewise, each of us can be like beggars, and we would give our right arm if we could be admitted and accepted—if we could just belong.

There are many forms of exclusion in which we may feel shut out at certain ages and stages of life. We may be excluded from certain economic groups because we are too poor or excluded by the poor who do not trust us or by our peers who are in competition with us. We may be excluded by a different generation, younger or older, who do not trust us or who do not understand us. Sometimes, we are excluded from our own selves because of interpersonal compartmentalization or because we have closed the door on some wounded area of life that we do not intend to open for fear of being hurt again.

As a means of coping with potential hurt, compartmentalization has some serious implications for those who practice it constantly. The walls we build to shut out hurt can easily become a cage and a temporary trap. This emotional hide-and-seek seems relatively harmless as long as we are in charge of the situation—as long as we are the "keepers" of our various identities—but the danger ultimately lies in self-deception. Few, if any of us, can pretend very long with human relationships without soon forgetting who we really are. Self-identity is a priceless possession that we need to navigate the stormy seas of life. To be shut out from knowing who you are is to lose the sense of where you are going. Identity is the chart and compass for life. To lose identity is a frightening experience that can produce odd and hurtful behavior.

I recently received a letter from a young friend whose life has been laced with painful experience. She wrote to me after a divorce from an agonizing and unsuccessful marriage. One key sentence from her letter sums up the dilemma. "Now that it is all over," she wrote, "I can finally get back to being myself— *if* I can remember who that is." The possibility of losing a sense of who we are is often easier and more subtle than we think. Of all the different kinds of alienation, the most painful and the most dangerous is alienation from parts of our own life, which usually results in the loss of identity.

There is a growing school of psychotherapy that maintains that we get healing from our hurts by a process of self-disclosure. This approach says that we get individual and social acceptance when we are willing to open up the closeted areas of our lives and share our hurts with others. Who knows how to help us unless he knows where we hurt? How can they know where we hurt unless we talk out our true feelings? There seems to be something redemptive and healing in the process of self-disclosure. There seems to be something helpful in our being willing to be truthful about the historical and festering hurts in our lives. In the context of the Christian faith, we would refer to this as prayer and confession. It's amazing how pride can create walls around us!

There are some shortcuts to acceptance and belonging in which you can be very subtly shortchanged. I see people frequently who are hurting because they have paid too high a price for a low quality of acceptance. In their desperate longing for belonging they pretend to become someone other than themselves in order to achieve the acceptance of some person whose acceptance is important to them. During the 1976 Bicentennial, there was a gold medal that sold for forty dollars. Somebody took the time to measure the gold content of the medal and found that it contained only twelve dollars worth of gold. I meet people almost every day who have made that sort of emotional transaction in their hope of buying belonging. Eventually they will discover that they are operating on an emotional deficit.

This sort of transaction has a predictably negative effect. The words and the music go something like this: I want you to love and accept me, so I begin to do all the things I know that you like, even when it cuts across my real feelings. I sacrifice who I am and what I really feel so you will love and accept me—so I will have a sense of belonging. You may not expect this sort of behavior of me at all. You would probably accept me just as I am, warts and all, but I am unwilling to take that chance. So I pretend. This little game soon results in an image that you take to be genuine and real. The mask soon becomes a cage. If I let down my guard and begin to let my real self show, all who have accepted my pretended image will begin to say: "What's wrong with Tom today? He is so unlike himself." I hurt, but I dare not show it. I am sad, but I must not cry. I am angry, but no cross word may pass my lips. For if I show how I really feel and who I really am, you may not accept me. I live in a lonely world behind a painted grin. What I have pretended to be is accepted, but behind this facade is the real me—isolated, alienated, and one step farther from acceptance than before this transaction started.

Have you ever been in a trap like that? I hope you haven't, but I'll bet you know someone who has. How many divorces have taken place because this was the kind of game that was played during courtship? How many clubs and various organizations do you know that have been created lately by lonely, alienated people who are trying to create some place to belong? I have often seen people who could not even pray with sincerity because they have pretended with people so long that they can't be honest with God. Edward R. Sill's jester in his poem "The Fool's Prayer" is required to be happy even when he is sad:

> The Royal Feast was done; the King
> Sought some new sport to banish care,
> And to his jester cried: "Sir Fool,
> Kneel now, and make for us a prayer!"
>
> The jester doffed his cap and bells,
> And stood the mocking crowd before;
> They could not see the bitter smile
> Behind the painted grin he wore.
>
> He bowed his head, and bent his knee
> Upon the monarch's silken stool;
> His pleading voice arose: "O Lord,
> Be merciful to me, a fool!"[2]

---

[2] Edward R. Sill, "The Fool's Prayer," *The Complete Poems of Edward Roland Sill* (Boston: Houghton Mifflin, 1906). Used by permission of the publisher.

A fool! And what fools we are to try to buy belonging, to purchase acceptance at the price of identity. For what does it profit a person if he gains all the acceptance and friendship of the world and yet loses his soul—his identity—in the transaction?

I am going to tell you a secret that took me forty years to learn. In fact, it took me so long to learn it that I am still trying to learn to practice it. The sooner you learn it the more quickly you'll be able to obtain and sustain a sense of belonging. This is what I have learned: people will admire and respect you for your correctness, expertise, and strength, but people will identify with you, love you, and have a sense of oneness with you when you let them see your faltering mistakes, hurts, and weaknesses. People will love you and let you into their world when they discover that you are human, as they are. If you hide your humanity with a sophisticated veneer of correctness, pride, and strength, you will never be admitted into the sacred inner sanctum of the lives of people. If you have a longing for belonging, learn to be who you are. Don't let pride stand between you and God or between you and other people. Admiration and respect are fine, but there always comes a time when you would trade all of that for just one little bit of genuine love, acceptance, and belonging. All of us are instinctively afraid of people who have never made a mistake, people who are always correct. Learn that lesson about life as soon as you can. You'll be glad you did. Barriers between you and others will dissolve if you can quit pretending that you're perfect.

Psychologically and theologically, many problems lie in store for those who seek acceptance through pretension. The word that Jesus came to bring is that God accepts us just as we are. We need not pretend that we are better than we are or other than who we are. Since God accepts us as we are, we ought to move through life with the hopeful expectation that people will accept us also.

The loving acceptance of God in Christ will give us such a sense of belonging where it really counts that we can survive any kind of rejection.

Handling Hostility

Psalm 4:4; Ephesians 4:25-27

A woman was bitten by a dog suspected of having rabies. She was rushed to the hospital, treated, and left in a room to wait for an autopsy report on the dog. Only then would she know whether she might have rabies. An intern on duty that day thought he should explain the seriousness of the situation to the woman. She asked him a lot of questions, and by the end of the interview the intern realized that he had told her more than he intended to tell her. She was visibly shaken. Later when he came by to look in on her, she was sitting on the side of the treatment table, writing. She would pause occasionally, stare out into space, then resume writing. The young doctor was sure she had upset her so much that she was writing her will or funeral instructions or some other equally grave document. He went back in to try to calm and comfort her. He asked if she were writing her will. "Oh no," she said. "Just in the event I have been infected, I'm making a list of the people I want to bite before I die."

Hostility is one of the most basic and most dangerous problems in all of life. Learning to handle hostility creatively is a lifelong task from which none of us is delivered. The abrasive forces and frictions of life generate in each of us a certain amount of negative feeling every day. This feeling accumulates if it is not immediately discharged or otherwise handled. This accumulation can cause an untimely and inexplicable explosion of anger. Have you ever had the experience of sliding from under the steering wheel of your automobile on a cold day and getting a surprising jolt from static electricity the moment your foot touched the ground? Sometimes sparks are visible at your fingertips, and a familiar crackle is heard. I always look around to see who did it, only to realize that I have been the victim of a very natural phenomenon. The electricity had built up in me then was discharged all at once when I touched the ground. I always think that I will be more careful next time.

The experience of everyday life builds up negative feelings, and we are sometimes shocked when something insignificant momentarily grounds us, and we find ourselves exploding in a manner that is entirely out of proportion with the situation at hand. There are many ways in which we handle resident hostility. Some people accumulate hostility and then explode. Some vent their feelings by slamming doors and kicking inanimate objects. Some people do a slow boil all of the time; they are perpetually like Mount Vesuvius just before an eruption. There are others who develop a skin rash, ulcers, or some other physical manifestation of their hostile feelings. Some sublimate their hostile feelings by perpetual righteous indignation in a never-ending series of crusades and causes. These are the people who need a public cause on which to expend their private hostility. Still others veil their hostility in sarcastic, sweetly worded phrases that cut like a stiletto. Then there are people who have learned how to express their feelings to the person who provoked them on the occasion of the provocation. They also express these feelings in a manner and to a degree in keeping with the magnitude of the situation. If I have left out of this brief list how you handle hostility, it has been unintentional. There are many ways in which people consciously or unconsciously choose to handle the hostility invariably generated by daily life.

Hostility is a normal part of human existence, and until we accept our humanity we are ill-prepared to deal with our hostility creatively. Unless there is a healthy expression of hostility, we are headed for a plethora of personal and social problems. Humankind is basically committed to conflicts. We may sublimate this need for conflict in a variety of vicarious experiences, such as football, war movies, television violence, and hunting, but hostility is for real.

Much of the information recorded in the four Gospels about the life and teachings of Jesus has to do with how to handle hostility. Not only did Jesus often deal with hostility, he also dealt with it in a final way. He had an inimitable way of communicating with people across the choppy waters of hostility. Not only do we see Jesus dealing with the hostility of others, but we also see him handling hostility in himself. What did he do when he was hostile? Did he store up his feelings and later abuse his disciples or kick the dog at Mary's house or abuse people who were defenseless? No. He confronted the source of the hostility at the time of its appearance. The most memorable occasion of Jesus' anger was when he threw out the money changers and cleansed the temple. Standing in the shadow of the cross with the weight of the last days heavy on him, he manifested a low-frustration tolerance for the greedy people who were exploiting so much that was sacred and so many who were innocent. Jesus dealt directly with his feelings, venting his hostility on the persons who provoked it, on the occasion in which it occurred, and to a degree consistent with the magnitude of the situation. Jesus not only handled hostility, he was also hostile—and he handled that also.

The two extremes of handling hostility uncreatively, repression and unbridled expression, can be seen all about us—and sometimes within us. Perhaps the most common symptom of repressed hostility is depression. For fear that the expression of our negative feelings will cost us dearly in terms of rejection by people we need, we become depressed instead of becoming angry. We turn our anger inward instead of outward. Unless the underlying cause of our anger is resolved, the depression persists. There are many other emotions we manifest when anger seems dangerous. We become tense, anxious, bored, or we may develop certain physical difficulties of a psychosomatic nature. In our culture it is much safer, in terms of security, to be depressed, tense, anxious, bored, or even sick than to be angry. Psychosomatic ills are probably more prevalent than most of us realize, even in ourselves. Since it is most difficult to distinguish between emotionally based physical difficulties and those that are strictly physically based, it is always wise to get immediate medical attention. "There is no question about the place of hostility in the creation of illness," says Carroll Wise, "when combined with anxiety, guilt, and shame, as it usually is, hostility presents a condition in which the human body and mind functions only with difficulty, or drives a person almost beyond the limits of his strength. Thus tensions, in various combinations, are present in much physical illness, through their power to inhibit or over-stimulate organic functioning. Here the hostility is unconsciously expressed through some organ of the body, or finds expression through other distorted forms of behavior, or irrational ideas.''[1] That is devastating, isn't it? But this is why and how hostility is dangerous.

The other extreme in response to anger is unbridled expression. It is seen best in the desire for revenge or in the veiled threat that ''God will get'' your enemies. One day a little girl came in from the school playground after recess, crying as if she were terribly hurt. The teacher asked her if she were in pain. The child said that she wasn't. ''Then why are you crying?'' the teacher asked. The little girl sobbed, ''Susan hit me, and the bell rang before I could hit her back.'' Revenge is a poor substitute for forgiveness in a civilized society.

Is there some bitter conflict in your heart that you have never resolved? When the fires of resentment smoulder in the soul, our minds turn instinctively to trying to ''get even.'' Jesus said that everyone who is angry with his brother or sister is in danger. There is simply no way to get comfort out of resentment and hate. Unresolved hostility is virulent. Hating someone is like burning down the barn to get rid of the rats.

The futility of revengeful hostility becomes obvious when we see how everybody is hurt and nobody is helped. A farmer, whose watermelon patch had developed an unwelcome popularity with the neighborhood kids, put up a sign: ''One of these watermelons is poisoned. Guess which one.'' The next day he found another sign next to the original that read: ''There's *your* poisoned watermelon, and there's *ours*.

---

[1] Carroll A. Wise, *Psychiatry and the Bible* (New York: Harper, 1956), pp. 95-96.

Now you guess which one." The personal and social implications of hostile revenge are frightening. Jesus said: "So if you are offering your gift at the altar, and there remember that your brother has something against you, leave your gift there before the altar and go; first be reconciled to your brother, and then come and offer your gift" (Matthew 5:23-24).

It is interesting to note that while the Bible records numerous incidents of killing, only two suicides are recorded. Saul fell on his sword, and Judas hanged himself. It is unusual that a history of so many people over such long periods of time would result in such a small incidence of suicide. But there is a logical explanation. Suicide is basically inverted hostility—hostility turned back in on oneself. It occurs most frequently when an intensely hostile person is unable to direct his hostility outward on something or someone. Among other reasons for the infrequency of suicide among Jewish people who dominated the biblical scene was their ability to express hostile feelings. The Bible is replete with passionate people who give expression to their feelings with relative ease.

In no place in the Bible is this characteristic more obvious than in the book of Psalms. Psalm 73. is a classic example of a person who is able to be "honest to God" about his hostility. It's the story of one man's hostility and how he handled it.

He has deep feelings of long standing that have deteriorated to hostility. The psalmist says: "I was envious of the arrogant, when I saw the prosperity of the wicked" (Psalm 73:3). He finally lays the blame for his situation at the feet of God, which likely means that he has had his turn at being hostile toward people already. He reproaches himself for trying to be decent in view of the indifference of God in the matter. "All in vain have I kept my heart clean and washed my hands in innocence" (verse 13). He has not spoken to others of his resentment toward God. Yet, when he tries to understand the matter, he comes up blank. There seems to be no alternative to a head-on confrontation with God himself. So, he saddles up his donkey and rides straight to "the sanctuary of God." He goes in a bitter and resentful man; he comes out reconciled and grateful. The text does not give us the benefit of knowing what was said, but we see the before and after scene very clearly. Being "honest to God," even in anger, is redemptive.

I do not mean to try to tell you precisely how to handle each particular hostile situation. It is difficult to give general advice about emotional problems because of the endless number of adaptations a human personality may make that are unique to that person. Prescriptions for emotional ills are therefore as highly individualized as the malady. For this reason "emotional patent medicines" are dangerous at best. Recurring strong feelings that get out of control often and disrupt personal relationships and bodily functions require the professional help of people who understand the intricacies of the human personality and know how to repair damaged emotional circuits. Beware of quick, simple, and all-encompassing solutions to deep-seated emotional problems of long standing. Some of them may sound as good as LSD, but they are just as dangerous. They can blow your mind! Take the emotional problems you cannot handle to people who by reason of training and experience are prepared to deal with them. When a problem is once removed from its source and the surrounding feelings are displaced on persons or situations that do not seem to be connected with the problem, it takes more than sincerity and a few verses from the Bible to deal with that problem successfully and redemptively.

To be angry is to be human. To allow anger to fester and deteriorate into hostility is to endanger both soul and body. You may check your emotional health—and normalcy—by making a list of the people you would like "to bite before you die" and checking to see if they are the same people who were on the list last year. Then check to see if the reasons are the same. If the persons and reasons are the same year in and year out, you are in danger. If the people and the reasons change frequently, you are relatively normal. If the list is short and frequently without names, you are growing in grace.

Both the Bible and life experiences counsel care in handling hostility. No human emotion is more common or more combustible. Be careful! Anger is like fire, which can be used to cook a meal or to burn down a house. Don't let your anger see the sun set. When you are angry ask God to guide you—and he will.

Climbing Invisible Fences

Matthew 6:25-34

There is an unforgettably profound scene in John Steinbeck's novel *The Grapes of Wrath*. The Joad family is on its way to California along with thousands of others, looking for a better life in a land they've never seen. Jim Casy, a former preacher and a troubled person, is traveling with them. When their ragged old car breaks down, Casy begins to pour out his doubts to Tom Joad about this seemingly jinxed rush to California. Tom resists Casy's pessimistic predictions with the simple answer: "I'm still layin' my dogs down one at the time." "Yeah," says Casy, "but when a fence comes up at ya, ya gonna climb that fence." "I climb fences when I got fences to climb," Tom replies. Casy just shakes his head and says, "It's the bes' way. I gotta agree. But they's different kinda fences. They's folks like me that climbs fences that ain't ever strang up yet— an' can't he'p it."[1]

Does that sound like anybody you know? To most of us, it

---

[1] John Steinbeck, *The Grapes of Wrath*, 2d ed. rev. (New York: The Viking Press, 1966), p. 237.

is a most familiar sound—and a familiar feeling too. In the secret councils of our souls, anxiety, in some form, is nearly always an agenda item. What is that invisible enemy of the soul that rears its ugly head in so many forms? It bleeds life of happiness and reinforces our most irrational fears. We may not be able to define it, but cope with it we must, for it is part and parcel of life. Our task is to plan not a life-style in which we are never anxious but a life-style in which we handle anxiety creatively. To live is to experience anxiety. Only the dead are without anxiety—and even that is an assumption of the living.

While it is correct to say that to be alive is to experience anxiety, it is also equally true that not all anxiety is creative and not all anxiety is alike. Paul Tillich, the theologian, makes a distinction between destructive and creative anxiety. The first is pathological anxiety, which is a neurotic and an uncreative response. The second is existential anxiety, which arises out of our very nature as human beings. Pathological anxiety is a disproportionate response to a real or an imagined situation—an illness that needs treatment by a physician. On the other hand, our existential anxiety is normal—a proper feeling that exists in proportion to a threatening situation. Anxiety is a part of our nature and existence as human beings, but it is to be confronted and conquered by the resources of our faith.[2]

When anxiety is acute, and when we cannot trace the feeling back to some situation or event that could or should have caused it, we need the skillful help of some person who by training and experience can help us.

---

[2] Paul Tillich, *The Courage to Be* (New Haven: Yale University Press, 1952), pp. 35-76.

The good advice of well-meaning friends and the preachments of the clergy are not adequate for treating pathological anxiety. So, let us consider the treatment and confrontation of existential anxiety—normal, human anxiety that usually expresses itself in nonproductive worry but that has not deteriorated to a pathological state.

Much anxiety arises out of our failure or our inability to accept our own nature as human beings. We have unrealistic expectations of ourselves, and we become anxious and guilt-ridden when we cannot meet those expectations. We expect perfection of ourselves, but we are so obviously imperfect. We have limited knowledge, limited strength, and limited understanding. We experience feelings that we cannot completely control. We are not paragons of virtue, courage, or love. In other words, we are not perfect—we are human beings. So, if we cannot accept our nature and our limitations, we are doomed to a high level of existential anxiety, and we are probably heading toward pathological anxiety.

During the Korean War, a chaplain was in a foxhole with two soldiers when the enemy threw a hand grenade at their feet. The chaplain instinctively picked it up and threw it back. The explosion killed two enemy soldiers. It was a devastating experience for the chaplain. He was virtually overcome with anxiety, guilt, and grief. It was the old master sergeant who finally brought him to his senses. He shook the chaplain and said, "Father, before you were a priest you were a human being." No matter what kind of veneer we use to civilize our nature, underneath it we are fragile, uncivilized human beings. And that veneer is much thinner than most of us would like to admit. If our expectations

40

dramatically deny our nature, our existential anxiety may soon deteriorate to pathological anxiety.

One of the earliest sources of anxiety in life is the fear of losing persons we love and who love us. Psychologists tell us that one of the earliest fears of a child is the fear of loss or separation from one or both parents. Severe family arguments are often devastating to little children because they are afraid that one of the their parents will go away. We never really get over this fear. Anxiety concerning the loss of persons who love us and upon whom we are dependent can be seen at almost any age and stage of life.

In the fourteenth chapter of the Gospel of John, Jesus deals with the anxious fears of his disciples who are upset because he is going to leave them. They have felt the warmth of his love. They have come to depend on him, and the possibility of life without him is the source of great anxiety. Jesus reassures them of some aspects of truth that are essential if they are to survive his departure with the kind of creative and dynamic faith with which he wants to leave them. This event is so basic, and the need to which it is addressed is so basic, that we can appropriate Jesus' reassurance for ourselves in our own existential anxiety. He says, "Let not your hearts be troubled; believe in God, believe also in me. . . . When I go and prepare a place for you, I will come again and will take you to myself, that where I am you may be also" (John 14:1-3). "I am the way, and the truth, and the life" (verse 6). "I will not leave you desolate; I will come to you. Yet a little while, and the world will see me no more, but you will see me; because I live, you will live also" (verses 18-19). So you see, Jesus offers ressurance of his continuing presence with them. He gives the disciples information that is essential yet

incomplete in detail. He asks the anxious little band of
followers to accept what he tells them and to trust him for
what they cannot see or understand. Anxiety then is to be met
with such truth as we have and with confidence in the
integrity of one who knows all truth.

Sometimes we become anxious because we wonder if we
are the only ones who are suffering from anxiety. But just
look around you. Most of the people with whom you will
brush shoulders today are somewhat anxious and a little
afraid. They, too, are beset with embarrassed concern that
they might be the only people on the street who are having
"problems with their nerves." There is anxiety behind the
pinched faces and furrowed brows of friends and acquaint-
ances everywhere. In some lives these burdens are handled
well, in some lives they are handled poorly, and in some, the
burdens are not really handled at all.

There is also another dimension to anxiety. Sometimes we
become vaguely anxious about the vast unknown that we call
the future. Ralph Waldo Emerson put the matter into clear
perspective when he wrote:

> Some of your hurts you have cured,
> And the sharpest you still have survived,
> But oh what torments of grief you endured
> From evils which never arrived!

When faith runs thin we begin to ask for a sign for proof, but
we would settle for some reassurance. The vague dread of the
unknown future causes us to imagine and fear about things
that we think *might* happen. Thomas Carlyle said: "Our main
business is not to see what lies dimly at a distance, but to do
what lies clearly at hand." We spend much energy climbing

fences that are not there, in a future that has not yet arrived. Jesus cautioned: "Do not be anxious about tomorrow; tomorrow will look after itself. Each day has enough troubles of its own."

By implication, the Lord's Prayer steers us around uncreative concern about the future. We are counseled to pray, "Give us this day our daily bread." The Lord's Prayer is a "now" prayer. The past is to be treated as the past, finding its sense of completion in forgiveness. The future is in God's hands. The legitimate time frame of human concern is now. Give us *this* day our daily bread.

For many of us, worrying seems to be our favorite indoor sport. Admittedly there are problems of such magnitude that they deserve our genuine attention and concern. But worrying is not a creative way to handle a problem. What can we do about chronic worrying, gnawing anxiety over trivial matters or over matters about which we can do nothing? There are some constructive things that we can do.

Worrying is a habit that can be controlled by conscious effort. If there are certain times of the day or certain conditions and circumstances under which you are more likely to worry, discipline yourself by refusing to worry during those particular times. Tell God that you are leaving all your worries in his hands during those special times. You may soon discover that this is a safe and wise thing to do. But this requires conscious effort.

Consciously lay aside some of the worries and burdens that you are carrying. There are matters and concerns that should be laid aside at the end of the day and should not be picked up the next morning. These consist of such things as harsh words spoken that cannot be recalled and irrevocable acts that cannot be amended or changed. I still remember a fable I learned in childhood. Two men were required to carry a handful of twigs from one place to another each day. One of the men refused to lay down the past day's supply of twigs. Each day his burden grew heavier, until finally he broke beneath the load. His companion happily deposited each day's supply of twigs in the proper place and with empty hands took the next day's supply. This is a parable of life. If we cannot lay aside the worries and concerns of yesterday, we will soon break beneath the load. There is an Oriental proverb that says, "My skirt with tears is always wet, I have forgotten to forget." If we cannot lay aside the mistakes and disappointments of the past, we will soon be unable to deal wisely with the problems of today. Consciously lay aside the unnecessary baggage of the past. Each day has enough worries of its own.

Another suggestion is to organize your anxieties. Deal with your worries one at a time. The great pyramids were built by placing one stone at a time. Break up your total anxiety package into small manageable units. This can be done by conscious effort. There is a large, four-drawer filing cabinet in my office that weighs more than three hundred pounds. One day when I was rearranging my office, I asked my son to help me move the big filing cabinet across the room. We could not budge it. My son suggested that we remove each of the drawers, move the empty frame, then replace the drawers one at a time. Since that day, I have been able to move the filing cabinet alone.

An overpowering burden of anxiety can be handled creatively if we will learn how to do it. Break it up into manageable units. Jesus did not promise us a life free from anxiety, worry, and burdens, but he has offered us a way of handling the inevitable anxieties of life. As Jesus put it, "Take my yoke upon you, and learn from me; . . . for my yoke is easy, and my burden is light" (Matthew 11:29-30). Remember that you must make a conscious effort to break your anxiety load into manageable units.

Learn to share the burdens that cause your anxiety with those who in love are willing and able to help you bear the load. We all need to be a part of some fellowship of people who care and with whom we can share our worries, burdens, anxieties, and concerns. Paul advised the people at Galatia to "bear one another's burdens" (Galatians 6:2). Tell somebody how you feel. Tell someone where and how you hurt. A shared burden grows lighter. Remember, it takes conscious effort to have the courage to share your anxiety. But it will help.

Not all anxiety is amenable to prepackaged prescriptions. Some anxiety is so deep and complicated that only the skill of a good physician of the emotions can untangle it. If you find yourself climbing fences that are not there, first decide whether you need professional help. If you do not, begin to exercise some conscious effort to deal with your anxiety with your own resources.

Jesus speaks of faith as the only effective antidote for fear and anxiety. Faith is not a commodity available to the casual religious person who treats God like a cosmic errand boy. We build a reservoir of faith by constant practice. We must believe and fail and succeed until trusting God becomes a natural response in all circumstances. When we accept Jesus Christ as Lord of all of life and not just a pilot for inclement weather, our faith will then enable us to live with anxiety in a creative manner. Until we can do this, we will continue to fight a losing battle with our fears and anxieties, and our nervous stomach will keep score.

There are plenty of real fences in life that we have to climb. Our biggest challenge is to recognize those invisible fences "that ain't ever strang up yet" and to ignore them. Sybil Partridge wrote a hymn that we would do well to remember in our struggle to creatively face the anxieties of life.

Lord for tomorrow and its needs
I do not pray;
Keep me, my God, from stain of sin
Just for today.

Living in Two Worlds

John 1:35-39

Picture the following scene in your mind: John the Baptist is standing with two of his disciples when Jesus walks past. He speaks a spontaneous tribute to Jesus: "Behold, the Lamb of God." John wasn't speaking to his disciples, but they heard what he said. They were intrigued, and they followed Jesus. Apparently they were too shy to approach him. Then Jesus did a beautiful thing, which was entirely characteristic of him. He turned and spoke to them. He broke the ice. He asked, "What do you want?" I doubt that they knew what to say, but one of them finally asked, "Master, where do you live?" I can just see a knowing smile creep across Jesus' face, as he said to the two timid disciples, "Come and see." They went home with him and stayed the rest of the day.

"Master, where do you live?" Well, just where did Jesus live? As far as this world was concerned, he didn't live much of anywhere. He lived like the rest of the peasant people in his time. He lived in a house with a dirt floor, lighted by an oil lamp. From his parables, we assume that he knew what it meant to wear patched clothes. Remember when he spoke of the folly of sewing a piece of new cloth to a piece of old cloth? We also know that there came a time in his ministry when he had no place to live, for he said to a potential follower: "Foxes have holes, and birds of the air have nests; but the Son of man has nowhere to lay his head" (Matthew 8:20). As far as this world is concerned, Jesus really didn't live much of anywhere.

Maybe these two bashful disciples already knew about his living arrangements. But they were asking a deeper and more profound question of Jesus. Their real question was, "Master, where do you live deep down inside? Who are you really?"

Jesus seldom told much about himself. The few times he identified himself in the New Testament are highly treasured and carefully studied. One of the self-ascriptions we know best is from the fourteenth chapter of the Gospel of John where Jesus said of himself: "I am the way, and the truth, and the life." The late Leslie Weatherhead, a great English pastor, wrote a book about the self-ascriptions of Jesus, which he aptly entitled *Over His Own Signature*. In that book Dr. Weatherhead pointed out that the Greek word, *aletheia,* which we translate into English as "truth" in John 14:6, also means "sincere." It is a word that conveys "revealedness." *Aletheia* suggests an open, continuing revelation of God himself in the person of Jesus Christ. We might translate that passage, "I am the way; I am the truth; I am sincere; I am the life." The word "sincere" would certainly be an accurate description of what we know about Jesus.

Dr. Weatherhead goes on to remind us of the origin of the word "sincere." It comes of two Latin words, *sine* (without) and *cera* (wax). It is really a word from the building business of ancient Rome. When marble pillars were made, there might be a flaw in one of them. Unscrupulous dealers would fill the flawed spot with wax. After polishing the wax, it looked just like the marble. Bad weather and the hot sun would eventually reveal the flaw. The owner of the building would then protest that the pillar was *non sine cere*, not without wax. When you write a letter and conclude by saying "I am sincerely yours," you are really saying "I am yours without wax." You claim that your relationship is genuine. It will bear the test of time and will weather the storm of life. You claim that you are what you appear to be.[1] Yes, we might well quote Jesus as saying of himself, "I am the way; I am the truth; I am sincere: I am the life."

The question the disciples put to Jesus was, "Master, where do you live?" He lived in one world of truth and sincerity. He is who he appears to be, and he will not melt away or disappear when life gets stormy or hot. He will not change. Jesus seemed to have a real thing about truth and sincerity. If there was anything that caused the Master to "lose his cool" it was hypocrisy in any form. He reserved some of his strongest statements of distaste for those whose outward show of piety was but a sham and a facade. He called upon all who followed him to live in one world of truth and sincerity. His call is still a challenge to us today as we struggle for individual wholeness in a world of duplicity.

The book of James in the New Testament reminds us that the double-minded person is unstable in all of his ways (see James 1:7). We were made for wholeness and unity, and any time we try to be more than one person or live in more than one world, the fragmentation begins to destroy us. The temptation to duplicity is often born of our desire to be all things to all persons. Sometimes we seek acceptance by pretending that we are someone or something other than who

---

[1] Leslie D. Weatherhead, *Over His Own Signature* (Nashville: Abingdon, 1955), p. 61.

49

we really are. Soon we forget what is pretended and what is real, and we lose our identity. Any time we are accepted for something we pretend to be, the acceptance is as hollow as the pretension. Ministers see more of this unholy pretension, or get caught up in more of it, than most people. Lay persons sometimes place ministers on a pedestal and pretend they are a little lower than the angels but not quite human. Unfortunately, we ministers often enjoy being put up on a pedestal, so we go along with the game and pretend to be the neutered creatures that people picture us to be. The halos on our heads get as big as hula hoops, and our true self-identity gets lost in the exchange.

Often when I am traveling I don't identify myself as a clergyman. Many people treat you very strangely when they discover that you are a minister. The fastest shift I have ever seen in conversation takes place with most people when they discover the ministry to be your profession. They begin to speak in a stained-glass voice, which is an octave higher than usual. All profanity ceases, and they start quoting things to you. (They think it is from the Bible, but it is usually from the old *Farmer's Almanac.*) I was on my way home on a plane once when I had a fascinating experience—which happens to me often. I sat in the back of the plane with the stewardess. We talked and had a marvelous and jovial conversation for about forty minutes. Then she asked me that inevitable question: "What kind of work do you do?" I knew it would end the freedom of the conversation, but I told her anyway. When she learned that I was a minister, I could tell what she was thinking by the look on her face: "Now, Lord, what all have I said?" She spent the last fifteen minutes of the flight taking back almost everything honest she had said up to that time. And the last time she served beverages, she didn't give me the same choices that she did the first time. People do strange things to you when they find out that you are a clergyperson. No one sees or becomes involved in more pretension than ministers. But, the truth of the matter is that God does not expect us to pretend before him or to one another. Jesus lived in one world in truth and sincerity, and he calls upon each of us to do the same.

Jesus calls on us to live in this world—the world of today. While it is true that we are only pilgrims, we are called to a relevant and meaningful pilgrimage by becoming involved with the affairs of this life. Religion sometimes lends itself to becoming an escape from the painful realities of life. Under the pressure of tension and anxiety, we may be temped to flee from reality by a return to the past or by trying to escape into the future. The past should inform and inspire us. We need to be aware of the past. The future should challenge us. We need to invest ourselves in the future by hope and faith. But the prominent thrust of our life energy should be toward living meaningfully today—right now.

There was a man who lost a fortune in business while he was away serving his country during World War I. During the 1920s, he rebuilt his business, which he lost again in 1929. After the great economic depression he regained his fortune. By that time, he saw war clouds of World War II gathering on the horizon in Europe. He told his family that he could not go through the trauma of losing another fortune. Sick and tired of the pressures of life, he sold everything that he had and decided to seek out some quiet place to spend the rest of his life. In the late 1930s he bought a ship and a map of the South Pacific. Determined to get away from it all he selected a remote island on that map and set sail for it. There he hoped to live out the rest of his years in happiness and peace. The name of that island was Guadalcanal. There is no way to escape the realities of life. Jesus calls us to live in *this* world—and, by his power, to redeem it. You might ask yourself the question that the disciples wanted Jesus to answer: Where do *I* live?

The disciples also had a question about the future. Jesus taught us that we would go on living forever. The idea of eternal life lies at the very heart of the Christian faith. While Jesus did not spell out the details of eternal life, he proclaimed it as a certainty. He spoke of the life that is to come just as if it were as real and natural as the life we know here and now. I believe this! There is not a shadow of doubt in my mind about it.

There has been a strong, healthy interest in death and life after death in the last few years. Elisabeth Kübler-Ross, a prominent psychiatrist who has studied death and dying for several years, said bluntly to a college audience: "I know beyond a shadow of doubt that there is life after death. It is no longer a matter of belief or opinion." Dr. Kübler-Ross came to this conclusion as the result of years of study and research with dying patients. It gives me great satisfaction to hear someone say "I know this is true," based on research and study. In the Christian church we have been proclaiming this truth for almost two thousand years. The authority by which we make this proclamation is that of faith and confidence in the word and promise of Jesus Christ. Here we see a meeting of scientific research and religious faith confirming the Christian promise of life after death. It does us good to have confirmed what we know to be true.

It seems a little ironic that two peasant disciples of twenty centuries ago were following Jesus, asking the same questions that you and I are asking as we follow Jesus today: "Master, who are you, where do you live, and what can you tell us about the mysteries of life so that we will not be afraid?" These are questions characteristic of those who must live in one world but who are, in a real sense, citizens of two worlds. We are citizens of this earthbound existence, but our ticket is made out to carry us to another world. The gospel story of the incarnation of God in Christ is the key to our dilemma. Living in two worlds is a neat trick—and only the incarnate God can make our sojourn on earth meaningful and the hope of our ultimate destination real. In the historical Jesus we see God breaking into time and history in the first century, and, through the proclamation of the Word he came to bring, we experience his saving presence in our life and in our world in the twentieth century.

"Master, where do you live?" Jesus lived in one world of truth and sincerity, and he calls us to do likewise. He lived in the world, and he calls us to relevant life under his lordship in the world today. He has preceded us in his death and resurrection, and assures us that he is preparing a place for us. In him we have the promise of living forever.

Our Trouble with Grief

John 11:32-35; Luke 19:41

In his book *Reflections on the Human Condition,* Eric Hoffer wrote: "A man's heart is a grave long before he is buried. Youth dies, and beauty, and hope, and desire. A grave is buried within a grave when a man is buried."[1] When I read Hoffer's statement, I was reminded of the doleful evaluation of life given by Job when he said, "Man that is born of a woman is of a few days, and full of trouble" (Job 14:1). I also remember Shakespeare's Macbeth who, because of life's unending sorrows, said:

> Out, out brief candle!
> Life's but a walking shadow, a poor player
> That struts and frets his hour upon the stage
> And then is heard no more: it is a tale
> Told by an idiot, full of sound and fury,
> Signifying nothing.
>
> (act 5, scene 5, lines 23-28)

A person's heart is a cemetery long before he dies. Life itself is freely sprinkled with grief and sorrow. From the time we are born until the day of our death, we experience a series of events and conditions that cause grief. We grieve the loss

---

[1] Eric Hoffer, *Reflections on the Human Condition* (New York: Harper, 1973), p. 88.

of childhood, innocence, youth, beauty, strength, desire, ambition, and hope. In a mobile society the onward flow of life continually brings losses that cause grief. We change jobs, move away from familiar surroundings, and are forced to break relationships that have formerly sustained us within. We suffer, and we see suffering. We disappoint, and we are disappointed. Death deprives us of friends and loved ones. And ultimately, we must face and grieve our own death, with all the fears and apprehensions surrounding that event. Even the most pessimistic persons do not overstate the prevalence of conditions and events in life that cause grief. But the pessimists, and many of us who do not claim that description, vastly underestimate the resources available to us all in times of grief and sorrow. But unless we find some satisfactory way of handling sorrow and expressing grief, we will be overcome by the natural events of life.

Jesus said: "Blessed are those who mourn, for they shall be comforted" (Matthew 5:4). A first reading of that blessed promise from the Beatitudes almost immediately makes us think of promises that have to do with some godly comfort we are to receive after death. And surely this is true. For we read with great hope in the Revelation of John that in the new Jerusalem, God shall be with his people, and "he will wipe away every tear from their eyes, and death shall be no more, neither shall there be mourning nor crying nor pain any more, for the former things have passed away" (Revelation 21:4). Surely God in heaven will comfort those who mourn of every sorrow that earthly life has inflicted. We grieve with the sure knowledge of the gentle comfort from God in the future. But what about right now? What about the days and years of this earthly pilgrimage? Is there some comfort we can find here and now other than the blessed hope of what is to come?

Our main trouble with grief is our failure to express it. Like any other emotion, grief will not disappear when suppressed. Grief is an emotion that is difficult to define. It is an agony of mind and heart that is more painful than any bodily affliction. The purpose of grief, in whatever way it is expressed, is to deal with that pain. To try to bypass the emotional stress of grief is to prolong the pain and delay the cure. "Blessed are those who mourn, for they shall be comforted"—right now.

Yes. There is comfort, healing, and release in the very process of the open expression of grief. One day I came home and found my ten-year-old daughter home from school before noon. I could hear her in the bedroom crying, and I could hear her mother coaxing and urging her to cry, and get it all out. Parents do not usually have to encourage children to cry. But, after I learned what was behind it all, I came to realize the wisdom of the coaxing from a mother who understood and cared. We had moved just three months earlier from a town where our children were very happy and well adjusted. The loss of friends and familiar surroundings was more traumatic than I had realized for my ten-year-old. She developed headaches at school that were immediately relieved when she walked in the front door at home. She was hypercritical of everything and everybody. We had not realized why until she came home from school that morning. When her mother asked why she had come home, she burst into tears and said, "I want to go home." "But," her mother replied, "you are home." "No," she said, "I want to go back to where we used to live. I want to go back where my friends are."

There are many normal losses in life that cause grief.

Perhaps we tend to regard these losses too lightly when they happen to others. And we often feel ashamed to grieve when they happen to us. How important it is to openly and verbally express grief and disappointment. There *is* comfort and healing and release in the very process of expressing grief. "Blessed are those who mourn, for they shall be comforted."

No matter what the sorrow may be, it must be grieved before it can heal. Until a sorrow is grieved it will keep coming back to sadden and depress us. Sometimes old sorrows that should have long since disappeared will return to haunt us in strange and unhealthy ways because we have not grieved that sorrow. Little do we know the extent to which scars of past wounds and the unfinished grief of significant losses flavor the quality of life.

Failure to grieve and give up what we have lost can cause strange and inappropriate behavior. It can cause physical difficulties for which the doctor can find no physical reason. It can create emotional pain for which there seems to be no cause. It can cause depression, hostility, and guilt. It can confuse one's identity and cause behavior that is very inappropriate for that age or occasion. For example, why will an old man with snow on the roof, or with no roof at all, begin to act and dress like a teen-ager and consider himself to be God's gift to the opposite sex? Why will a woman who is thirty-nine and holding, but who would pass for sixty, begin to act coy and flirtatious? Likely, they have not grieved and given up the loss of their youth. They have not faced up to and properly grieved the disappointments of an age and stage of their life that is obviously gone forever. Blessed are those who grieve what is lost, for they are then free to move on to what is ahead.

There is prevalent in many of us the deep-seated feeling that it is wrong to express grief or, if not wrong, that grief is an expression of weakness. I have often seen parents urge their children not to cry about something that should naturally provoke grief. How often I have cringed to hear a well-meaning friend say to someone who had lost a loved one, "Buck up and trust the Lord and don't cry." We tend to ascribe strength, courage, and deep faith to people who show no expression of grief in the face of situations where grief is appropriate. What a gross injustice we do to encourage people to bottle up their natural feelings of grief. We would do them a far greater service to encourage them to cry or do whatever best expresses grief for them.

I cannot help remembering that Jesus not only said, "Blessed are those who mourn, for they shall be comforted," but Jesus also wept. The New Testament records two occasions upon which Jesus wept. He wept when he looked out over the city of Jerusalem and realized that they were not going to accept him and that the city would be destroyed. It was the death of a city and the death of a person that brought him to tears. When Jesus returned to the village of Bethany, Martha met him to tell him that Lazarus was dead. Lazarus' other sister, Mary, was in the house, lost in her grief and sorrow. Jesus sent for her. She came weeping and fell at his feet and said, "Lord, if you had been here, my brother would not have died." When Jesus saw her weeping, he was deeply moved. Then the Bible says very bluntly: "Jesus wept" (John 11:32-35). If it was important for Jesus to weep, how much more should we weep and grieve our sorrows and losses.

There is a passage of scripture in the Old Testament book

of Isaiah that is understood to be a description of the Messiah who was to come. When we study the earthly life and experience of Jesus, it is easy to identify him with that messianic passage in the fifty-third chapter of Isaiah. He is described as "a man of sorrows, and acquainted with grief" (Isaiah 53:3). It gives me great comfort to know that Jesus, in whose name I offer my prayers, knows how I feel when I am grief-stricken and brokenhearted. There is no hurt that can come to me with which Jesus is not sympathetically acquainted. When you grieve the losses that life inevitably brings, you do not stand alone in your sorrow and tears. God, in Christ Jesus, knows and understands and weeps with you. You can trust in him. "Cast all your anxieties on him, for he cares about you" (I Peter 5:7).

How we handle grief is wrapped up in our understanding of the nature of God and the problem of evil. I have heard people say, "It doesn't matter what you believe as long as you believe something." This is not true! It always matters what we believe, for out of our philosophy and belief come our actions and attitudes. It is true, however, that we should not try to counsel people about what to believe while they are experiencing some specific sorrow. We would do well to try to think through some biblical and rational understanding of sorrow long before sorrow comes. Several years ago Leslie Weatherhead wrote a very helpful little book entitled *The Will of God*. It was written out of his experience of being the pastor of City Temple in London during World War II. Dr. Weatherhead developed a concise and understanding philosophy of suffering and sorrow that does not indict God and that offers great relief for those for whom grief is necessary.

How we handle grief has much to do with our understanding of the nature of God. The Christian understanding of the nature of God, as we see him in the life and teachings of Jesus, gives an entirely new understanding of suffering and sorrow. It is important to teach our children that adversity is not a punishment for our sins. Our children should learn early in life that God will not lead us around sorrows but that he will walk with us through them. If we understand God to be like Jesus, we can find great comfort from our faith in times of trouble. We can grieve our losses and openly express all of the feelings that surround that grief. We can unload the guilt attached to the event and avoid further feelings of guilt because we have grieved.

We should become familiar with death and illness early in life. It is also important for our children to learn that sorrow and adversity are real. Many parents try to protect their children from the realism of death by not allowing them to see dead persons or to attend funerals. Children should attend some funerals before the death of a close loved one slams them hard against a wall of reality about death.

The strength with which to handle adversity and creatively grieve losses is born of a nurtured faith. It does not come to those who look for it only when they need it. It does not come to those who disregard the disciplines and patterns that open our lives to the kind of faith God wants us all to have. None of us can pull faith out of a vacuum. It must be planted, nurtured, tested, and given a chance to grow. The victory that we see in the Cross was won in the wilderness, in the retreats of prayer, and in the Garden of Gethsemane.

There is a real sense in which we find victory over adversity because we trust that God will see us through it all.

There is great power in a faith that holds on to hope even when the ground upon which we stand is wet with tears. Harry Emerson Fosdick preached a sermon at Riverside Church in New York entitled "The Power to See It Through." He concluded his sermon with a testimony to the power of the resources of the Christian faith to see us through the inevitable adversities of life. "I celebrate the resources of the Christian faith to see a man through. If faith in God means such things, how do men live life through without it? How do they meet the shocks of fate, the ugliness of evil, the shame of man's inhumanity to man, the disheartenment of moral failure, the impact of personal sorrow, and still keep their morale? I celebrate the resources of the Christian faith."[2] There comes a time in which we must put on the whole armor of God if we are to face life's battles victoriously. Like Paul, we must learn a kind of resilient faith that allows us to be beaten down without being downcast, to be discouraged but not defeated, and to grieve but not lose hope. Experience teaches us that grief is like a long, winding valley, where around most any bend may appear a totally new landscape. William Cowper, the hymn writer, once wrote:

> Sometimes a light surprises the Christian while he sings;
> It is the Lord, who rises with healing in his wings.
> When comforts are declining, he grants the soul again
> A season of clear shining, to cheer it after rain.
>
> In holy contemplation we sweetly then pursue
> The theme of God's salvation, and find it ever new;
> Set free from present sorrow, we cheerfully can say,
> Let the unknown tomorrow bring with it what it may.

---

[2] Harry E. Fosdick, "The Power to See It Through," *Riverside Sermons* (New York: Harper, 1958), p. 36.

It can bring with it nothing but he will bear us through;
Who gives the lilies clothing will clothe his people, too;
Beneath the spreading heavens, no creature but is fed;
And he who feeds the ravens will give his children bread.

Sometimes a shining light surprises. Through glistening tears we can find God coming to meet us in Christ Jesus, our Lord. Francis Thompson wrote a poem entitled "In No Strange Land" that witnesses to this experience, using his own personal sadness as the subject and the familiar surroundings of London as the setting.

But (when so sad thou canst not sadder)
Cry;—and upon thy so sore loss
Shall shine the traffic of Jacob's ladder
Pitched betwixt Heaven and Charing Cross.

Yea, in the night, my Soul, my daughter,
Cry,—clinging Heaven by the hems;
And lo, Christ walking on the water
Not of Gennesareth, but Thames!

"Blessed are those who mourn, for they shall be comforted"—in this world and in the next.

You Can't Go Home Again

Luke 9:57-62; Genesis 3:24

The towering figure of Thomas Wolfe moved like a giant across the backdrop of American literature until his death in 1938. This colorful and talented North Carolinian was a man of conflicts and extremes, all of which seemed to give him grist for writing in a manner that touched the deep needs of people. He wrote a novel that was more autobiographical than imaginary entitled *You Can't Go Home Again*. He deals with his own personal sorrow and deep disappointments in his writing. It is the story of George Webber, a man who, early in life, succeeds beyond his fondest expectation. Like Alexander the Great, he conquers all that was known in his field while he was very young. But Webber soon learns the startling truth that fame and fortune do not offer ultimate satisfaction. He decides to go back to his home in Asheville, North Carolina, to recapture some of the simple and innocent joy of his youth. Traveling back, he dredges up old memories, long stored up and much embellished. He has erased memories of ugliness and unhappiness much like an artist alters unpleasant tones and lines in a picture. But the moment he steps off the train, his dreams and rose-colored memories begin to crumble beneath the weight of cruel reality. It has all changed—tragically so! Then the truth dawns on him—the way back to yesterday is closed forever. Wolfe wrote: "He saw now that you can't go home again—not ever. There was no road back." Thomas Wolfe discovered a truth written into the constitution of life: the fact is that none of us can ever really go back home again.[1]

Most of us are ardent lovers of the past. Nostalgia plays a major role in our lives. We love the past because we are familiar with it. And even when we have bungled some aspect of the past, we create a myth about it to make a pretty picture in our minds. We love the past because we have some hesitation about the unknown factors of the future. The older I become, the more difficult I find it to accept the changes that life inevitably brings. I do not like change. I have noticed this about myself since I have been "thirty-nine and holding." If I had my way, I would want my son to be seven years old and my dog still a puppy. But life treats such wishes with cruel disregard. No one and nothing stays like it used to be. Things keep growing and changing, and I have to adjust.

Recently, I found myself falling prey to the errors of age when I tried to explain to my children at Christmastime how much more they were getting for Christmas than I got when I was a child. I was waxing eloquent about the matter, engaging in gross hyperbole (which is a seventy-five-cent word for lying). Then I noticed the look of sympathetic disbelief in the eyes of my children. It snatched me back to reality—at least for the moment.

---

[1] Thomas Wolfe, *You Can't Go Home Again* (New York: Harper, 1934), p. 704.

The good old days take on a grandiose mythology, but in our more thoughtful moments, we know it really isn't so. The most ancient and revered book in our Christian tradition is a living witness against the viability of nostalgia. Page after page of the Bible teaches us that you can't go home again. Jesus spoke eloquently of the folly and the ultimate disloyalty of putting one's hand to the plow and then looking back. He saw this as more than a casual glance and more like a life-style and a stance. Not only is this true of the life and witness of Jesus, it is true of the most ancient pages of this ancient book.

A fitting example is the beautiful story of Ruth in the Old Testament. After the death of her husband, Ruth insisted on leaving Moab and going to the land of Judah with her mother-in-law, Naomi. Naomi urged her to stay in Moab. In classic words of undying loyalty to her husband's people, she said: "Entreat me not to leave you or to return from following you; for where you go I will go, and where you lodge I will lodge; your people shall be my people; and your God my God" (Ruth 1:16). Ruth knew that she could never find happiness in going back. She knew that you can't go home again.

There is a passage in the Old Testament book of Genesis that tells how Adam and Eve were cast out of the Garden of Eden and how the Lord God placed a guard with a flaming sword at the gate to keep them from returning. God was saying: You can't go home again—you can't go back to where you have been; that gate is shut and forever sealed. Any return to the past must be through fantasy and memory.

From the beginning, God has been trying to point us toward the future and to save us from the past. This truth is etched into such classic stories as that of Abraham, who journeyed on, knowing not where he was going. Remember also the story of Lot and the destruction of Sodom? The Lord decided that he could not live with the sins of Sodom, but before he destroyed it, he allowed Lot and his family to leave with the understanding that they were not even so much as to look back. The Bible describes in graphic language what happened to Lot's wife when she could not let go of the past. The writer of Genesis said, ''Lot's wife behind him looked back, and she became a pillar of salt.'' You can't go home again! The past hardens, atrophies, and finally destroys the person whose eyes are not set on the road ahead! Don't look back!

Jesus once tried to go back home, but he found the experience so disappointing that he commented, ''A prophet is not without honor, except in his own country, and among his own kin, and in his own house'' (Mark 6:4). By precept and example, Jesus taught us that life, both here and hereafter, is an ever-growing and expanding process that builds upon the yesterdays but never lives there. Our richest experiences and our deepest insights are to be found on the unfamiliar terrain of today and amid the unknown experiences of tomorrow. You can't put your hand to the plow and look back, else while enamoured with the familiar past, you will miss what is just ahead. The Bible plainly and painfully teaches us that you can't go home again.

Life itself is also an eloquent witness to the truth that you can't go home again. Our emotional makeup is such that a constant return to the past tends to weaken us. When by choice or inability, we fail to grow beyond a stage of past development, we suffer from a condition the psychologists call fixation; that is, we get hung up on a snag and cannot develop normally. The child who continues to suck his thumb beyond the age when thumb-sucking should stop is fixated. The child who insists on carrying his blanket around with him beyond a certain age is fixated on a security symbol. Charles Shultz, in his "Peanuts" comic strip, has classically illustrated fixation in his character Linus. He makes us see ourselves in the kids he creates. Someone asked Linus what he was going to do about that blanket when he went to college. He said, "I plan to have it made into a sport coat." Many of us have adapted our fixations to make them appear socially acceptable. Many are still "on the bottle" at thirty-nine. The only difference is that it now has a cork instead of a nipple. Many still have their pacifiers, except now they are filter-tipped. We don't have temper tantrums as we did when we were children, but we do rant and rave with righteous indignation. Do you by chance have some fixation that you have turned into a sport coat—that you have doctored up so it will be socially acceptable?

Fixation in the human personality is stagnation, a desperate return to a former level of development in order to avoid the anxiety of the unknown present or future. There is also such a thing as spiritual fixation; I know because I have seen it. As embarrassing as it may be to say so, I know because I have experienced it in my own life. I have tried to live on past blessings. I have gone back to drink from wells of experience that have long since gone dry. I have become so preoccupied with how and when and where and at what time I was saved twenty-eight years ago, that I became oblivious to my need for God to keep on saving me. John Wesley once said:

I have been saved.
I am being saved.
I will be saved.

The late William L. Stidger, once head of the preaching department of Boston University School of Theology, used to enjoy telling of his courtship with a young lady named Minnie Hood. As a young man, Dr. Stidger was madly in love with Minnie Hood. She was a ravishingly beautiful creature. He was so much in love with her that at times he did irrational things. On one occasion, when he visited her, she was saturated in strong-smelling perfume. When he learned that his rival had given the perfume to her, he demanded that she show him the bottle. He took the bottle from her and emptied the contents in the yard. Then he went to the drugstore and bought her another bottle just like it. But, for some reason not disclosed, Dr. Stidger never married Minnie. Some years later—in fact, forty years later—Dr. and Mrs. Stidger went to Spokane, Washington. After getting settled in a hotel, Dr. Stidger turned rather casually to his wife and said, "I think I will go out and see Minnie this evening." Mrs. Stidger thought that was a fine idea, and so he went. When he reached her home, his heart was beating like a trip-hammer. For forty years he had carried around in his mind a mental picture of that beautiful creature, and now he was about to see her again. The door was opened by a woman who weighed no less than two hundred and fifty pounds. Dr. Stidger groped, stared, and stammered. Yes, it was Minnie. When he returned to the hotel, he told Mrs. Stidger how terrible Minnie looked. His wife gently replied, "William, did you ever stop to think what a shock that wrinkled face and bald head of yours must have been to Minnie?'' You can't go home again!

Each autumn I try to prepare the youth from my church for the great shock they will get when they come back home on their first visit from college. They look forward to getting home, but home is not like what it used to be. Everybody has changed, you have changed, and things are not the same. You visit the high school where you graduated, and all the kids look young and act immature. You go back to your old hangouts and see people you don't even know. Gradually, you begin to know for sure—you can't go home again, ever! You have to go forward because the road back is closed.

Recently I went back to the place where I was born and reared. I am still shocked that things are not as I remembered them at all. The pathway from the house to the barn is not a mile, only about a hundred yards; the swimming hole, which I thought was oceanic in size, is but a small place in the little creek; and the pasture isn't five miles from the barn, it's just over across the road by the edge of the cotton field. When these childhood memories turn out to be distortions of recollection, it sometimes leaves a sense of sadness because we wish it was as we remembered it to be. Thomas Hood, in his poem, "I Remember, I Remember" gives us a meaningful sense of this feeling.

> I remember, I remember
> The fir-trees dark and high;
> I used to think their slender tops
> Were close against the sky:
> It was a childish ignorance,
> But now 'tis little joy
> To know I'm farther off from Heaven
> Than when I was a boy.

We love the comfortable feeling of things being as we remember, but life keeps confronting us with truth that relates to reality as it is now. Life teaches that you can't go home again, and when we learn that lesson, we will have passed one of the first tests of maturity.

The church and its history of experience says you can't go home again. We tend to get nostalgic about religion, perhaps more quickly than about anything else. And nothing kills the meaning of true religion more quickly than nostalgia in the church. It was the bane of Jesus' whole ministry, and it was essentially those who were fixated on the good old days who crucified him because he kept disturbing their myths. The church keeps looking for a safe place to fixate itself in the past, but God keeps showing us new commitments that require us to let the dead bury the dead, and move on. James Russell Lowell reminded us of this when he said:

> New occasions teach new duties;
> Time makes ancient good uncouth;
> They must upward still, and onward,
> Who would keep abreast of Truth.

The church can never go back. History and tradition mark out clearly the nature and task of the true church. Ancient victories inspire us, and old errors rise up to warn us. As George Santayana once said, "Those who cannot remember the past are condemned to repeat it." Errors and all. But, in our proclivity to nostalgia, our greatest danger does not seem to lie in our ignorance of history but in our rigid obsession with it. We are incurable lovers of the familiar and romanticized past. And in a cataclysmic day like ours this romanticizing can be fatal. Our cry for the "good old days," so we can do things like they used to be done, is not an affirmation of the faith of our fathers. It is a rejection and a denial of it. Our forebears did not live out the faith in what was to them the "good old days." They struggled by faith with the uncertainty of their own time. Things never were like they used to be for them—and things will never be like they used to be for us. Our heroes of the faith were children of their times, but they were not prisoners of history. If they had been, they would never have become our heroes in the faith. One could hardly imagine Jesus, Martin Luther, or John Wesley as champions of tradition. Can you imagine Jesus saying, "What we need to do is get back to the good old days"? And what about John Wesley? Can't you just hear him saying, "Now, Charles, let's sing some of the good old-fashioned hymns and quit confusing everybody with those new-fangled tunes that you and Isaac Watts have been writing"? We dare not try to go back into the past. Whoever saw a bird go back into the shell, a butterfly back in the cocoon, or Christ back into the tomb? Oliver Wendell Holmes, once walking on the beach, picked up a shell where a mollusk had lived. Examination revealed that each spiral made a larger compartment to accommodate the mollusk as it grew. As the little creature outgrew one chamber, it had moved to the next—a larger one. From this experience he wrote the famous poem "The Chambered Nautilus." The concluding verse reads:

> Build thee more stately mansions, O, my soul,
> > As the swift seasons roll!
> > Leave thy low-vaulted past!
> Let each new temple, nobler than the last,
> Shut thee from heaven with a dome more vast,

'Til thou at length art free,
Leaving thine outgrown shell by life's unresting sea!

You can't go home again. The Bible, life, the church—all three teach us this lesson. We would be wise to learn the lesson well.

The Heavy Shoes of Death

John 14:1-10, 15-18

The death of a person close to you is a frightening experience. All of us avoid and deny death. It makes us feel uneasy. But eventually we will have to deal with death. We understand death for the first time when it puts its hand upon one whom we love. How will we handle the sorrow? Sorrow comes clothed in many different cloaks. But first and last, in one way or another, sorrow knocks on every person's door, and no pleading will turn it away. Sorrow is one of the common denominators of life, and sooner or later we all experience its leveling force.

No two persons experience sorrow alike. Sorrow takes on the particular flavor of the life in which it occurs. You may hurt and I may hurt, but you do not hurt the same way as I do. There is something basically unique in each person's sense of sadness, sorrow, and grief. All of our feelings are grounded and rooted in the unique factors that come together to compose life as we know it. It seems, however, that the more feelings tend toward sorrow and the deeper feelings run, the more private they become. We can share feelings of joy much more readily than we can share feelings of sorrow. Feelings surrounding sorrow are more frequently rooted in highly individualistic content, known and experienced only by the person in whose life these feelings occur. It is futile to try to comfort sorrowing persons without understanding the highly personal nature of suffering, sorrow, and grief. In order to understand feelings we must understand the person who experiences these feelings.

Life does not offer a deeper sorrow or a more painful reality than that of negotiating the eventuality of death. And yet there is no eventuality in life that is more certain. The English philosopher Francis Bacon said, "It is as natural to die as to be born; and perhaps one is as painful as the other." When sorrow walks with the heavy shoes of death, it brings a sadness from which even the most sophisticated and rational person cannot escape. Neither the power of positive thinking nor the recognition of the universality of death can minister to those strange feelings that well up in our souls when the dusty smell of death enshrouds us. We shudder at the thought of our own demise, and we identify hesitatingly with the demise of others. Death is a timely reminder of the frailty of human life.

All of us have some basic needs when someone near us dies. At the time of death we all huddle a little closer together, not in the hope of dodging death, but in the hope of finding some comfort and protection in those near us. We need the understanding and empathy of those we love and those who love us. We least of all need someone to tell us how to feel on the occasion of death. But we *do* need those we love and trust to understand how we feel and to help us understand the puzzling and unanticipated aspects of our feelings. When death comes it is too late for instruction because we will have already set the tone and quality of our feelings by our former experiences and understandings. Any time you wish to be of real help to a friend who is grieving, just listen. Listen to what is in the grieving person's heart. Listen with interest and without judgment. If you are asked a question, such as "Why did this happen to my loved one?" you would be well advised not to try to answer that question literally. The grieving person does not want you to explain why (even if you could). The question "why" on the occasion of death is a request not for information but for understanding. Let your response be to the underlying dynamics, and convey to that person your empathic understanding of the hurt and shock they feel.

When death strikes near us the effect of the shock is often unanticipated. It may leave the grief-stricken person numb and dazed. You may feel lifeless and listless. You may feel that all that is going on around you is unreal. Frequently, a grief-stricken person will experience an initial sense of hopelessness and despair. Only a deep sense of faith can help one see beyond the darkness of the moment. This sense of faith is not something that can be superimposed on the grief-stricken person. It must be the tested faith of the person who is grieving.

There are some things we need to understand about death and our response to it in advance of being faced by death. We need to understand that grief in its various manifestations is not a sign of a lack of faith but simply the legitimate means of expression of feeling that cannot be adequately expressed in another way. Some people place a premium on an unemotional, expressionless acceptance of death. This is a dubious virtue, more in tune with social expectation than with emotional health and realism. The expression of grief is often painful because it is born of pain, but to the extent that feelings of sorrow are present, grief expression is important and necessary. The person who negotiates death with a stone face, dry eyes, and no emotional expression will very likely have a delayed reaction to grief. The longer the delay between the event of death and the expression of grief, the more likely there is to be serious problems. We do well to remember that on the occasion of the death of a dear friend, Jesus wept. None of us are called upon to be stronger than our Lord. He knew what it was like to feel the sharp sword of death cut close, and he reponded with genuine grief. If anyone understands how we feel in the face of sorrow associated with death, it is Jesus.

We begin to formulate our understanding of death early in life. It is conveyed to us at home, at church, and at school. Children are confused if the reality of death is denied or ignored or hidden behind glib language, even glib religious language. It is proper to take the myth out of death and rescue it from gross pagan understandings. Our children would greatly benefit from an interpretation of the fourteenth chapter of John on the occasion of death. "Let not your hearts be troubled; believe in God, believe also in me. In my Father's house are many rooms; if it were not so, would I have told you that I go to prepare a place for you? And when I go and prepare a place for you, I will come again and will take you to myself, that where I am you may be also. And you know the way where I am going" (John 14:1-4). The reassuring quality of our Lord's words offers comfort for us all and puts forth a philosophy of death with which we can comfortably live. My children found meaning in Robert

Freeman's simple verse about death because they had been studying geography.

> When souls go down to the sea by ship,
> And the dark ship's name is Death,
> Why mourn and wail at the vanishing sail?
> Though outward bound, God's world is round,
> And only a ship is Death.

Fear of death is a basic human instinct by which we are preserved. Anyone who does not know the meaning of the word "fear" as it is associated with death perhaps does not know the meaning of many other words either. Several years ago, when I was a chaplain in the cancer ward of a hospital, a terminal cancer patient said to me, "I know I shouldn't feel this way, but I don't want to die." I replied, "How very human of you. I don't want to die either." The will to live is a basic human instinct. The Christian faith does not teach us to want to die; it teaches us how to face death.

Jesus said to the sorrow-ladened people of his time, "Come unto me, all who labor and are heavy laden, and I will give you rest. Take my yoke upon you, and learn from me; for I am gentle and lowly in heart, and you will find rest for your souls. For my yoke is easy, and my burden is light" (Matthew 11:28-30). Jesus did not mean that in his "way" there would be no burden. He meant that the burdens of life and death would be manageable. The Christian faith and way provides us with a means of negotiating burdens that make them light and manageable. Biblical scholars say that the Greek word that we translate as "easy" really means "fits well." This verse could well read, "For my yoke fits well, and my burden is light."

TIGERS IN THE DARK

I grew up on a farm in south Alabama during an era in which oxen were commonly used as beasts of burden. One of the main pieces of harness for oxen was a yoke. It was very important for the yoke to fit well, because all of the harness and the weight of the burden pulled against the yoke. A poorly fitted yoke would cause the animal unnecessary pain and would impair his working strength. The Christian faces death as does the heathen. The only difference is the way in which it is faced. "My yoke fits well," said Jesus, and that makes the burden light. That makes the difference when sorrow walks with the heavy shoes of death.

No one has expressed the faith we need more beautifully than Henry van Dyke in his poem "Voyagers."

> O Maker of the Mighty Deep
> Whereon our vessels fare,
> Above our life's adventure keep
> Thy faithful watch and care.
> In Thee we trust what'er befall;
> Thy sea is great, our boats are small. . . .

> When outward bound we boldly sail
> And leave the friendly shore,
> Let not our hearts of courage fail
> Before the voyage is o'er.
> We trust in Thee, whate'er befall;
> Thy sea is great, our boats are small.

> When homeward bound we gladly turn,
> O bring us safely there,
> Where harbour-lights of friendship burn
> And peace is in the air.
> We trust in Thee whate'er befall;
> Thy sea is great, our boats are small.

THE HEAVY SHOES OF DEATH

Beyond the circle of the sea,
    When voyaging is past,
We seek our final port in Thee;
    O bring us home at last.
In Thee we trust whate'er befall;
Thy sea is great, our boats are small.[1]

When we see someone we love round the bend in the river of life that we call death, only our faith can save us from fear. And when the working tools of life slip from our nervous grasp, and we ourselves move out into the unknown, only our faith can save us—and it will.

[1] Henry van Dyke, "Voyagers," *Thy Sea Is Great, Our Boats Are Small* (Old Tappan, N.J.: Fleming H. Revell, 1922), pp. 9-11.

Getting Rid of Guilt

Luke 5:17-26

Have you ever found yourself being uncommonly kind to persons toward whom you have actually felt hostile? Have you ever found yourself exploding with violent and inappropriate anger at innocent people in your own household? Have you ever realized that you were giving very stern and demanding advice about matters that are really a problem for you? Have you ever felt a burning sense of worthlessness, as if some strange hand had reached unbidden from the underside of your life and turned the dial of self-esteem back past zero?

If you can answer yes to any one of this limited list of guilt-symptom questions, you qualify for membership in the human race, together with all of us who live after the Fall. Guilt is perhaps one of the most common and one of the most complicated of all human feelings. Just what is the source and the nature of these feelings of guilt that gnaw us from within and ruin us from without? And what can we do about guilt?

From the earliest days of childhood we begin to build a set of standards against which we constantly, consciously or unconsciously, measure our behavior, feelings, and attitudes. This ever-growing image of what we ought to be is commonly called a conscience. This complicated piece of emotional equipment was once described by a little boy as being "the part of a person that takes up more room than all the rest of your insides put together."

The conscience is not selective about its content. It is built from whatever materials are available from the total input of one's emotional life. The human conscience may have some decidedly unhealthy aspects, some self-expectations that are more harmful than helpful. Nonetheless, our conscience is the standard by which we judge ourselves to be right or wrong in a given situation. When we violate this built-in set of rules, the result is a sense of guilt. We then perceive ourselves as transgressors. This sense of guilt may come as the result of behavior, attitude, or thought. Our conscience is a sort of internalized prosecuting attorney, which serves as an accuser when we violate our own standard of values. The conscience forever reminds us of the difference between what we are and what we ought to be. Guilt accumulates unless it is forgiven or disposed of in some way satisfactory to the conscience. The greater the accumulation of guilt, the more anxious, insecure, and unworthy we feel. We often become angry at ourselves for being less than we feel we ought to be, and then we become depressed. Our guilt, hostility, and depression not only make us miserable—they also play havoc with our relationships to other people.

What we commonly call conscience is sometimes oblivious to new information and insight about ourselves. The obstinate and dominating authority of the conscience with power to override reason comes from a psychological process called introjection. Sigmund Freud, the father of psychiatry and psychoanalysis, formulated the concept of introjection as a means of describing a condition that he found in many of his patients. Freud reasoned that there must be a long-term emotional process akin to the very familiar physical process of ingestion, digestion, and absorption of food. For example, a meal eaten in the evening is digested and absorbed by the body during the night. The meal becomes, in the process, a part of the body, permeating every area of the body to the fartherest extent of the circulatory system. Freud reasoned that an image, idea, or concept is fed into the emotional system of a child and, by repetition, is digested and absorbed into the child's emotional life. For instance, a nagging, guilt-inspiring mother with a martyr complex can eventually become a permanent mental fixture to a child who is exposed to it often enough and under the proper circumstances. Once that mother image is introjected, the influence of the image on the child does not depend upon the mother being physically present. Any time that child does something the mother doesn't like, although mother may be a thousand miles away and the child may now be forty years old, he feels guilty just as he did years ago when she was standing over him. She has been introjected, and neither distance nor death can remove her. The process of introjection also works in the same manner in response to favorable images and concepts. The older a child becomes, the less amenable he is to the process of introjection.

When I first read about the theory of introjection, it seemed rather farfetched. But when I reflected more carefully on my own early development, I discovered that it had happened to me. There were three cardinal sins in the little rural community where I grew up: going to the movies on Sunday, going fishing on Sunday, and doing any sort of work on

Sunday. There were other sins, to be sure, but we seemed to hear more about these three than any others. My parents, my church, and the community in general concurred in the culpability of those who violated those local unwritten amendments to the Fourth Commandment. I remember going fishing one Sunday afternoon with my brother. We caught several fine fish, which we proudly brought home to show to my father, thinking that our prowess in angling would offset any consternation about our moral lapse. That was a decided miscalculation! My father unceremoniously discarded the fish, and then he lifted me by my overall galluses until my feet were about three inches from the floor. When he set me back down a few minutes later, I *knew* that you were not supposed to fish on Sunday. His reaction greatly facilitated the process of introjection about fishing on Sunday!

When I left home to go to college, there were several things I had been wanting to do for a long time. One of those things was to go to a movie on Sunday. I will always remember my first experience with Sunday movies away from home. I went to the ticket window, looked up and down the street to see if anybody was looking, then darted quickly inside. I sat anxiously through what was supposed to be a humorous movie, and as I left the theater I looked both ways to see if the coast was clear before stepping outside. I thought I had left my parents, my church, and the little community where I grew up, but I had not. I had introjected them, and they were still right there with me. Logically, I see nothing morally wrong about going to a movie or fishing on Sunday, but to this very day I cannot with good conscience do either one. The human conscience is a strong and sometimes strange piece of emotional equipment.

With so much emotional equipment to monitor what we do and think, no wonder guilt is a universal human problem. But how do we handle guilt? There are some unhealthy ways of dealing with guilt we should be careful to avoid. Some people project their guilt onto other persons. Some people deny guilt—ignore it. And there are some of us who are good at rationalizing guilt. The truth of the matter is, when we rearrange the rules or make excuses for our failure to be what our set of values says we ought to be, this does not avoid, eliminate, or in any way handle guilt. It simply puts a blanket on our guilt and allows it to sink into our subconscious. Subconscious guilt manipulates our lives in a much more insidious manner than it would if it were conscious. From the core of our being, the guilt we have repressed or forgotten makes us sick in body and in soul. Our subconscious guilt controls us, but we cannot control it. Sometimes the guilt from our subconscious comes floating to the surface in a dream in which we feel helpless and insecure, but as soon as we awaken, we promptly repress it again by forgetting the dream.

Guilt is a normal by-product of daily living. It is not just a feeling that awaits some occasional specific act of obvious wrongdoing. To live is to experience guilt. The daily generation of guilt as a normal by-product of living is comparable to the more tangible process by which daily household life generates garbage. No matter how nice and sophisticated you are, you generate some garbage. Well-organized households develop a daily garbage disposal routine. In this manner the garbage problem is handled as it develops—daily. Can you imagine some person deciding that they are too nice to deal with garbage in their household? The problem of garbage might be kept hidden for a few days or a few weeks, but it would develop into a serious problem if ignored too long. Likewise, serious emotional and spiritual problems develop in the lives of people who do not learn how to get rid of guilt as it accumulates. The answer to the human problem of guilt is to be found at the heart and center of the Christian faith. Jesus died so we could know how far God is willing to go to forgive our sin and guilt and redeem us. In the cross of Christ we see God acting in our behalf, not just for that moment in history, but for all time. In Christ, we see God bridging the chasm to meet us where we are. The death of Jesus was not a sacrificial act on the part of humankind to soften the heart of a recalcitrant God, it is a sacrifical act on the part of God to soften the heart of humankind. As the Gospel of John puts it, "God so loved the world that he gave his only Son, that whoever believes in him should not perish but have eternal life" (John 3:16).

The New Testament teaches us that we are saved from our sin and guilt by the grace of God. Our good works cannot save us—they are not good enough. The good news of the gospel is *not* that Jesus taught us higher ethics. The Sermon on the Mount, if understood only as ethical standards for humankind, is not good news. It is bad news. There are times in which we have difficulty reaching the minimum ethical standards. It is not good news to be told that the standard has been raised, unless in the announcement some provision is made for our failure to reach it. The good news is that our Lord does not require us to reach a certain level of ethical attainment before he will accept us! He will accept us just as we are, guilty failure that we may be. Jesus Christ's attitude toward us is like that of a good doctor toward a patient. A good doctor does not require a patient to reach a certain level of health before he will treat him. He takes the patient just as he is, sick and debilitated, and begins to lead him back to health. Jesus accepts you. God accepts you. Your salvation from sin and guilt awaits your acceptance of the fact that God in Christ has already accepted you.

Thank God we don't have to carry around the "trash" of what we have been in the past. We don't have to try to sort, rearrange, hide, or cover up our guilt. God will forgive us our sin and remove our guilt. Once we are delivered from the guilt of the past, we need only to confess the guilt of each new day as it accumulates. We will never be guiltless, but we can all be forgiven. God is gracious and willing to forgive us and remove our guilt from us as far as the east is from the west.

There is a hymn we used to sing in the little church where I grew up that places the whole matter of getting rid of guilt in its proper theological perspective:

> Just as I am, thou wilt receive,
> Wilt welcome, pardon, cleanse, relieve;
> Because thy promise I believe,
> O Lamb of God, I come, I come!
>
> Just as I am, thy love unknown
> Hath broken every barrier down;
> Now, to be thine, yea, thine alone,
> O Lamb of God, I come, I come!

Only the Lonely

II Timothy 4:9-13

There is a popular song with the line, "Only the lonely know how I feel tonight." There may be some of you who have never been lonely, but I doubt it. Loneliness is a universal feeling that pervades everyone's life at some time. After you have regained meaning and identity, you find it easy to forget your lonely times. Forgetting unpleasant experiences is a fortunate characteristic of the human mind. But few of us, if any, go through life without knowing the pain of wistful loneliness of some kind.

What is loneliness? It is a kind of slow-moving, internalized tragedy. It is unspectacular disaster. Chronic loneliness frustrates us because there is usually no socially acceptable cause to which we can point and say, "See, I have been hurt here." So, an intangible and inexplicable feeling leaves an invisible wound. Thus the timid victim of chronic loneliness is further isolated by the feeling that no one can or will understand. Most of us know what it is like to be lonely, but don't know how to describe it. It is a feeling that defies verbal explanation. No one has come closer to offering some verbal context for understanding loneliness than Henry Wadsworth Longfellow in his poem "The Day Is Done." He depicts it in a few classic lines:

TIGERS IN THE DARK

I see the lights of the village
Gleam through the rain and the mist,
And a feeling of sadness comes o'er me
That my soul cannot resist.

A feeling of sadness and longing
That is not akin to pain,
And resembles sorrow only
As the mist resembles rain.

We see loneliness at so many ages and stages of life: the little
child with no real live playmates who creates imaginary
friends to fill the lonely void; the homesick college student,
trying to prove to himself that he doesn't have to go home
every weekend; or the widowed person whose children have
moved away, trying to find meaning amid all the reminders
of a happier yesterday. Slice into life at most any age or
place, and loneliness will be there in some form—or at least
you will see the scars where it has been.

Most people can negotiate the occasional lonely times and
places in life and comfortably recover. Unfortunately, there
are some persons for whom loneliness is not an occasional
event but a constant way of life. Occasional loneliness is
livable, but constant loneliness will kill the spirit of any
person who does not find some appropriate means of lighting
a candle to dispel the inner darkness that it brings. There is a
malignant loneliness that corrodes the soul, a pathological
loneliness that is untouched, much less cured, by verbal
assurances. There is a sick loneliness attached to psychic
scars that reflects emotional battles of the distant past.
Whether in victory or defeat, those encounters were costly,
and they still cost—the victory was pyrrhic and the defeat

malignant. This is the kind of loneliness we rightly fear and which, if we do not cure, will destroy us.

Loneliness is not only painful, but when it is constant and insoluble it can have a dangerously erosive affect on behavior patterns. The news media carry stories daily of crime, drug abuse, violence, and antisocial behavior by quiet and timid people whose sudden departure from the socially acceptable norm is inexplicably shocking to those who thought they knew them best. In more cases than we might guess, these are the desperate acts of lonely people who have reached the threshold of their endurance of isolation. Loneliness, isolation, and nonbelonging so convincingly confirm one's feelings of inadequacy, unworthiness, and unacceptableness that in a crisis one may well decide that nothing really matters because no one really cares. And when nothing really matters and nobody really cares, there are very few boundaries left.

Because of the very personal makeup of those for whom loneliness is a critical factor, few of them ever allow themselves to rebel against their lot in life unless they are pressed into a circumstance of spectacular crisis. The persons whose loneliness is chronic and malignant are more likely to perish from within, inch by inch, in quiet desperation. There are more intensely lonely people than you would ever dream for whom radio, television, and the newspaper provide the illusory solace of company. In *Escape From Loneliness,* Paul Tournier tells of a lady who worked in a busy office with people all around her each day but who would leave her radio on beside her bed at night and wait for the announcer to say, "And so we bid you a very pleasant good night." It was a real human voice speaking to her, and she needed that.

There are some around us who will clamor for attention

and get it. But those who most desperately need the touch of love and understanding are those who are quietly perishing for lack of love and attention. They seldom fill out cards at church in request of a visit or prayer. They almost never send word by way of whispered criticism arising from pastoral neglect. They do not write letters to radio and television preachers. They smile pensively, do what they are asked, continue to be self-effacing, and thus slowly perish in quiet loneliness. Only someone from outside—someone who is sensitive, someone with the bold courage to love and care—can break down the walls of their lonely spiritual prison.

Recently I read a free-verse poem by Donna Swanson entitled "Minnie Remembers." Two verses in the middle of the poem reflect the hurt of loneliness.

> How long has it been since someone touched me?
> Twenty years?
> Twenty years I've been a widow.
> Respected.
> Smiled at.
> But never touched.
> Never held close to another body.
> Never held so close and warm that loneliness
>   was blotted out.
>
> I remember how my Mother used to hold me, God.
> When I was hurt in spirit or flesh
> She would gather me close,
> Stroke my silky hair and caress
> My back with her warm hands.
> Oh, God, I'm so lonely! [1]

[1] Donna Swanson, "Minnie Remembers," in *Images*, comp. Janice Grana (Nashville: The Upper Room, 1976), p. 118. Reprinted by permission of The Upper Room.

ONLY THE LONELY

Where do we learn to be lonely? More than likely we develop this unhappy condition at the same place where we develop most of our basic feelings—at home. Many homes become a training ground for loneliness because there is no meaningful communication between members of the family. Where there is no meaningful communication between family members—no joys shared, no sorrows mutually borne—a child has loneliness built into his concept of life. A child thus learns the lonely way of life depicted by Matthew Arnold in his wistful little couplets:

> In the sea of life enisled,
> With echoing straits between us thrown,
> Dotting the shoreless watery wild,
> We mortal millions live *alone*.

The one-way communication of the mass media is a poor substitute for warm personal relationships between members of a family. It is frightening to see so many homes where television replaces conversation, where information is plentiful, but communication is nonexistent. Many children know more about Captain Kangaroo than about their own fathers and more about the adventures of fictional cartoon characters than about the daily lives of the neighborhood children. It is dangerous to have children identify with fictional persons and situations that have the illusory appearance of reality, while their identity with traditional molders of character, such as teachers, pastors, scout leaders, parents, and other relatives, is marginal, if existent at all.

Is your home a training ground for loneliness? Loneliness and aloneness are not the same. In the late evening of March 28, 1976, without fanfare, the world population reached four billion. The five billion mark is estimated for 1989, and by the year 2012 the world population could be eight billion. Where there are so many people, it seems inexcusable to be lonely. Despite all these people around us on this small planet, we still personally suffer an epidemic of loneliness. If loneliness and aloneness were synonymous, we would have no problem in a world with problems of overpopulation. The truth of the matter is that loneliness can be, and often is, an illness of persons who live and associate with the masses. We are lonely by ourselves, even when we are with other people. Sometimes we wonder if anyone would miss us or notice our absence if we did not show up tomorrow.

Even some of the busy, and seemingly happy, young people are not strangers to loneliness. Pensive music with lyrics that romanticize tragedy and dramatize loneliness seems to strike a responsive chord at a deep level in the younger generation. Many youth who fill their lives with a constant round of unrelenting activity perhaps cover up more loneliness than we would ever guess. New York psychiatrist Herbert Hendin, who has treated college-age students extensively, reports a 250 percent rise in college-student suicide rate in the past fifteen years.

Some people are lonely because they have consciously withdrawn from in-depth human relations. Past experiences of rejection and hurt have made them more afraid of love than the loneliness of life without it. They have made the tragic choice of withdrawing from emotional involvement rather than run the risk of being hurt again in an attempt to love and trust. This decision closes the main door to life and leads to pervading and constant loneliness. In our nomadic society, where most people move numerous times in a lifetime, many people are afraid to put down roots and make close friends because the pain of parting hangs over their heads like the sword of Damocles. With no close friends, no deep roots, loneliness becomes a natural by-product of this mobile society.

Whatever the source or extent of loneliness, the faith we espouse in Christ Jesus our Lord offers a solution to those who can and will appreciate it. Jesus came to show and tell humankind that God cares. It is through Jesus that we are saved—*from* many things, including loneliness, and *to* many things, including meaning. When I was a child, I used to hear my pastor talk about the saving knowledge of God, and I did not know what in the world he meant. I was a grown man before I understood that the saving knowledge of God is the simple and sincere trust that what Jesus told us about God is absolutely true—and that the seal of validation for that trust is in the Master's life and death and resurrection.

We know intellectually from our religious education that God cares for us, but this knowledge is rather difficult to assimilate into usable emotional comfort and spiritual reassurance unless we experience it in terms of human relationships. It is difficult to believe that "God loves you, and I love you" until the Word is made flesh in a real experience. The Christian church is in the caring business, so that the Word of God can be made real to the lonely and the lost.

From the dark and lonely recesses of prison the apostle Paul wrote his young protégé, Timothy, to come to him with haste. Demas and Crescens and Titus had left him. Only Luke, his physician, was there. Paul needed the presence of one who cared to authenticate his faith that God cares. Paul survived all the circumstances of loneliness and remained productive to the end because he knew that someone cared both in heaven and on earth. There is a real reason for those of us in the church to be sensitive to the unspoken needs of the timid and the inarticulate lonely.

The pain of loneliness has no physical equivalent, and this "grey ghost" is no stranger to any of us. The Bible tells us that even God was once lonely, and out of his loneliness he created humankind. God, help us with our lonely feelings. And he will!

Baffling Reflections

I Corinthians 13:8-13

It was more than twenty years ago, but I remember the encounter as clearly as if it were yesterday. I was a chaplain intern at Cook County Hospital in Chicago, assigned to the female cancer ward. As I walked into an anteroom on my ward, a young, beautiful woman was sitting in a wheelchair gazing pensively out the uncurtained window. I had been to see her many times before, but she had made little response to my visits. As I walked toward her chair, the accumulated information I knew about her flashed through my mind— early twenties, married, two small children. And then I was startled to recall the words and symbols on her medical chart that indicated terminal cancer. As I walked beside her, I saw that she was weeping softly. I stood silently a few seconds before she realized I was there. Then she began to talk as she had not talked before. She was talking to me, yet what she had to say was addressed beyond me. She spoke pleadingly, "I don't understand. Why doesn't God help me? Why? I don't mind waiting. I have been waiting for two years. When will I ever understand?" She sighed, a glazed look came into her eyes, and she waited for my response. *What would you have said?*

Who can answer these questions from the depths of the

human soul? Despite all my compassion and concern, I had no final answer. I had only myself to offer at that moment. Glib categories and pretty theological words are of no help when you get into that kind of deep water. Life does not drive us that deep very often, but when it does, we see things in a different perspective. Issues and concerns that we once thought important become of no concern, and things that were once of little concern become primary.

When we are put to the test, most of us discover that there are numerous areas of uncertainty about the realities of life. We want to understand how it all fits together. We want to make sense of the confusing patterns. But even with all our human information, logic, and reasoning, the confusing patterns will not come clear. The fact is, the real meaning of life and the reality of God is incomplete to our human eyes and our human ability to comprehend. We simply do not understand the meaning of all that we see. There is so much that seems incompatible with what we have been taught about the nature of God. The apostle Paul acknowledged this in the thirteenth chapter of First Corinthians when he said, ''Now we see only baffling reflections in a mirror.'' This may not make much sense if we think of the mirrors we have at home. We see whatever is reflected there sometimes with painful clarity. Corinth was the mirror manufacturing capital of the ancient world, but they had not learned to silver mirrors as we do today. Their best mirrors were made of polished metal, usually silver or bronze. These mirrors reflected only a dim image with all of the details blurred out. When he spoke of our understanding of life being like the baffling reflections of a mirror, the Corinthians understood Paul very clearly.

This is how it is with our understanding of God and the

reality of life. In our best moments we are willing to acknowledge our lack of exact knowledge and insight. We admit to this in some of our greatest hymns about God and life: "Holy, holy, holy! Though the darkness hide thee, though the eye of sinful man thy glory may not see." "Immortal, invisible, God only wise, in light inaccessible hid from our eyes." The dim voice of nature suggests that we live in an orderly world, made to be a place of beauty and peace. But then comes war, natural disaster, famine, and death, and the shadows begin to creep over the mirror of life. We want to believe that we live in a friendly universe where all things will ultimately fit together for good. We try to understand what is happening to us and around us. We try to understand the goodness of God against the backdrop of sin and suffering, natural evil and war. But in the end, we see only baffling reflections and a painful absence of clarity and unity of purpose.

We discover that we are not at all unlike those who lived before us. Even the best people of the Bible wept these same tears and asked these same questions. It was Job who, in his depth of sorrow, cried out, "Oh, that I knew where I might find him!" (Job 23:3). Even the psalmist, who could perhaps see life more clearly than most people, cried out in desperation, "How long, O LORD? . . . How long wilt thou hide thy face from me?" (Psalm 13:1). The apostle Paul had deeper insight than most any of the saints of old, but he admits the imperfect nature of humankind's deepest insights. We believe that we see God most clearly in the person of Jesus Christ. But even in Christ, the insights are not perfect or clearly defined. Great areas of concern are still unenlightened by his words and life. Jesus found that he was unable to explain himself as clearly and completely as he wished, even to his disciples. He said, "I have yet many things to say to you, but you cannot bear them now" (John 16:12). So despite the highest revelation of God in time and history and despite the subsequent working of the Holy Spirit to enlighten the lives of people, the picture is still incomplete and to a degree obscure like the baffling reflections of a mirror.

Different people draw different conclusions from the same baffling reflections. This is evidenced by the large number of different denominations of the Christian faith. Each of these denominations believe, at least to some degree, that they have the right interpretation of the baffling reflections. Even within these denominations there are varying degrees of difference of interpretation of the same evidence.

Each person sees life and interprets the baffling reflections in the light of and by the dictates of his own inner needs. A person's theological beliefs indicate far more about that person than most of us would ever dream. We appropriate from the vast storehouse of God's nature the part of his nature that we need. We begin with the dim outlines and baffling reflections and paint in the detail that speaks to us where we are. There will be those who will see and understand things about God that you and I will never see and understand. For who knows to what deep need God, in his wisdom, has spoken when we see people who are marching to a drumbeat that we do not hear? There will always be persons who have some insight that you do not have or who cannot see the brilliant light of insight that is so clear to you. There will always be those who believe what you believe more or less strongly than you. The extent of difference is not to be considered a measuring stick for error. We are persons not robots. Our needs are different and so are our insights.

We deduct from the dim and baffling reflections of revelation what we need in order to put our lives together with meaning. I went to the state fair with a friend recently. I would not say that my friend is fat, but his girth is such that he refuses to discuss measurements. We went in the house of mirrors. We found there mirrors that made us appear in whatever shape we would like to see ourselves. Can you guess in front of which mirror he stood the longest and admired himself the most? You are right, the one that made him look thin. He wanted to buy that mirror and take it home with him. We look for and usually find in life whatever speaks to our deep needs. We seek and we find in God the characteristics that speak to our deep needs. Those who feel guilty are attracted to the parts of the Bible that speak of God's forgiveness and mercy. Differences of understanding often reflect different needs and different life experiences.

How shall we understand God in his majesty and life in its mystifying intricacies? Let us imagine that we are going from America to England on a ship. Leaving from New York, we notice that the land mass can be seen through the shallow water. After traveling for a while, we notice islands of land jutting up from the water. Then we see a chain of islands. Approaching the harbor in England, we once again see that the land mass extends underneath the water. We might assume from the evidence we have seen that there is a connectedness between the land mass in America and the land mass in England. The land we see underwater on each side of the ocean and the mass of land in the form of islands at sea leads us to this logical assumption. *But* we do not know this to be true. In fact, there are many puzzling aspects of the theory if our data is limited to what we have observed. Our knowledge of the matter is incomplete, and we lack certainty. But suppose we meet a deep-sea diver who has been down to the ocean floor, who has walked on it and charted by instrument all upon which he has not walked. If he tells us what we believe about the connectedness of land mass is true, and if we trust him to be giving us correct information, then we can speak with confidence on the matter. Our power to reason about what we know, our capacity to fill in the blank spots in our knowledge, our confidence and trust in one who has been there—all of these things come together to make believers of us. Then, and only then, do we trust and believe the information. Then we feel we actually know and can accept our observations.

On the journey of life we see some evidence that leads us to believe, as Paul did, that "in him all things hold together" (Colossians 1:17), that "in everything God works for good with those who love him" (Romans 8:28). But sin and evil, suffering and death, bring shadows of doubt that confuse and frustrate us. Jesus Christ came into time and history to speak to us as One who has been there, as One who comes from God. He tells us that what we have hesitatingly believed is really true—that God does work for good with those who love him, that in God all things hold together. This is more beautifully and perfectly true than we can ever understand in this world. If we trust Jesus, if we believe him, then our knowledge is made complete by that faith. We can speak with assurance, not only because of our own experience, but because we know in whom we have believed. Faith in One who has been there is the only solution to the puzzling reflections that constitute life. Unless we can appropriate with confidence the saving knowledge of God as given by Jesus Christ, we are doomed forever to be lost in doubt and fear.

In the thirteenth chapter of First Corinthians, the apostle Paul acknowledges that we now understand life as if it were puzzling reflections in a Corinthian mirror. But he considers it self-evident that the time will come when the shadows will be pushed back, and we will see "face to face." When we round the bend in the river of life that we call death, our faith will be translated into knowledge and our prayers will become personal requests. As Paul says, "When the perfect comes, the imperfect will pass away" (I Corinthians 13:10). But, in the "meantime"—and we are now living in the meantime—we must fill in the dark places and the puzzling parts by faith in Jesus Christ, who came from God, the Father. Paul finds great comfort for himself and for the Christians in Corinth in the blessed hope that in time we "shall understand fully, even as I have been fully understood." Ignorance and mystery are on the side of humankind, not on God's side. I do not understand the answer to all the questions my mind poses, but thank God I trust in One who does. This is a saving faith for those who live in the "meantime," with a partial understanding of important areas of life.

Like the ocean, life is too large for us to know all about it by direct experience. Our widely spaced islands of limited knowledge cannot answer the deep mysteries of life. We do not know enough to trust knowledge. We will never know enough to trust knowledge alone. The very circumstance of our existence leads us to lean on One who has been there. It is in him, and in him alone, that all things hold together. We may not be dying of cancer, but like the dying patient we have unanswered questions about life in whatever circumstance we may be. And someday our need to know the answer, or to know someone who knows the answer, will be a life and death issue. The answer is to be found in our trust of him who said, "I am the way, and the truth, and the life. . . . Him who comes to me, I will not cast out." For those who will believe and obey him, whether they be wise or simple, he will reveal himself in the toils, the conflicts, the mysteries, and the sufferings through which they shall pass. He is our answer.

"For now we see in a mirror dimly, but then see face to face. Now I know in part; then I shall understand fully, even as I have been fully understood" (I Corinthians 13:12).

With how much mystery can we comfortably live and still be creative and purposeful people in God's world? How much must we know in order to feel secure? How much faith can we put in Jesus? The answer to that question may save us.

Taking a Chance on Love

Romans 5:1-11

In my years as a minister, I have seen many broken hearts. And in the finest sense of the word, broken hearts is my business. I don't know how to mend a broken heart. But I do know someone who can. By faith and hope, God can mend any broken heart if we are willing to bring him all of the pieces.

There are many ways in which brokenheartedness can occur. It could be the job that you thought should have been offered to you that was given instead to another person. It may be the honor you thought should have come to you that was given to someone else. It could be the person you loved who didn't return your love or the person you trusted who let you down. It might be the dream that became a nightmare or the hope that never materialized. There are a thousand ways to get a broken heart, and none of them are easy. But of all the broken hearts I have seen, there's one with the longest sting and the deepest hurt of all. It is the broken heart from loving and trusting someone only to find that, in one of the many ways in which rejection may come, you have been turned down—cold.

You take a chance when you love or trust or in any way offer yourself to another—the chance of whether your love, your trust, or you yourself will be accepted and affirmed. Have you ever offered to shake hands with someone who refused to shake hands with you? It is an unhappy experience. I have had this unfortunate experience twice in my life. I think everybody ought to have the experience once—but not more than once. It leaves a most peculiar feeling and illustrates rejection better than anything I know. There you are with your hand out, with no one to accept it.

When I was growing up, there was a popular love song about the risk of love and loving. The refrain was, "There I go again, taking a chance on love." The song had reference to romantic love, but the truth is, we take a chance when we love or trust at *any* level. Love is risky, whether it is at the level of romantic love or whether it ascends to that level of love about which Jesus spoke when he said, "Greater love has no man than this, that a man lay down his life for his friends" (John 15:13).

I have seen many people who have been hurt by rejection. They often pull a defensive iron curtain around their lives. Then they cannot reach out to others, and, sadly, others cannot reach in to touch them.

I have seen little children who, because of rejection by their parents, became so afraid of loving or trusting that only radical emotional therapy could save them from a completely loveless life. Once while I was a chaplain in a ward for disturbed children in Chicago, I encountered children too young to talk who had been beaten and rejected by their parents. When I would try to talk to them, they would turn their faces to the wall to avoid looking at me. It was as if they were saying, "No, never again. I have already been hurt by loving and trusting. I will not risk it again." Their rejection came so early in life and was so much of a part of what they knew life to be that they were unable to verbalize or understand what had happened to them. They were pathetically isolated from trust and love—perhaps for the rest of their lives.

I have also known teen-agers and adults who, when they experienced the pain of rejection, would withdraw from any and all relationships that might cause them to be tempted to love or to trust again. They were more afraid of the pain of love than the emptiness of life without love. It is perhaps to young persons that disappointment in love and trust is most likely to happen. The young are reaching out to establish their identity beyond the family. Seldom does a young person get through the years without being disappointed and hurt in some experience of love.

Before you decide that I am opposed to loving and trusting on the basis of the risk involved, let me assure you that I believe in trusting and loving. Let me remind you of a saying from Alfred Lord Tennyson that is so old that all of us know it and so true that none of us can ever escape from the truth of it: " 'Tis better to have loved and lost than to have never loved at all." Loving and trusting are so much a basic part of the fabric of life that the moment you cease to love and trust you also cease to live. Several years ago Smiley Blanton, an eminent Christian psychiatrist, wrote a book in which he described what happens when we cease to love and trust. The title of the book is not only an appropriate revelation of the contents but also an apt description of life. The book is entitled *Love or Perish*.

If I understand the fifth chapter of Paul's letter to the Romans correctly, Paul is reminding us of how Jesus Christ, our Lord, took a chance on love when he died on the cross. (Who could improve on Paul's exact language?) "While we were still weak, at the right time Christ died for the ungodly. Why, one will hardly die for a righteous man—though perhaps for a good man one will dare even to die. But God shows his love for us in that while we were yet sinners Christ died for us" (Romans 5:6-8). God took a chance on love!

God took a chance on love as the means of our redemption. Jesus risked rejection so that all of us could know how much God loves us. This is the saving knowledge of God. While we were yet sinners, while we were still indifferent, while we were unlovable, God took a chance on love to reach us. This is the final proof of the extent to which God is willing to go in order to redeem humankind. If we ever come to know dynamically what it means to be lost, it will be because we said no to a love like this. If we ever come to know dynamically what it means to be saved, it will be because we said yes to a love like this, that runs so deep and risks so much.

This is God's way with humankind. The very thought of God's persistent love reminds me of Edwin Markham's four-line verse entitled "Outwitted."

> He drew a circle that shut me out—
> Heretic, rebel, a thing to flout.
> But Love and I had the wit to win:
> We drew a circle that took him in!

This is God's way with humankind. He does not force his way into our lives, no matter how miserable life may become. But he always holds a cross before us as a constant reminder of his love and a symbol of his willingness to receive us back again.

There seems to be a universal hesitation in people today when it comes to an open and spontaneous expression of feelings. We are afraid to express negative feelings unless we are highly provoked. As strange as it may seem, we are equally afraid to express love and trust. Experiences of rejection have left sensitive scars on our souls. We are afraid of the commitment implied by love and trust. We are afraid of rejection by those to whom we may extend ourselves. Perhaps the most logical place to begin to correct this is at home. For until we can take a chance on love with those who are least likely to reject us, it is not likely that we will risk rejection by people outside the family circle.

The failure to communicate love and trust is one of the most serious problems in family life and in church life today. And until we can take a chance on love with people in the fellowship of the church, it is not likely that we will risk rejection by those outside the fellowship of the church. If we but knew how hungry people are to hear and feel some spontaneous expression of love and trust, we would be far less hesitant. It is a real sin to fail to express the positive feelings of love and trust that we have. If God was willing to risk his Son so that the world might know of his love, do you not suppose he might be willing to risk some of his sons and daughters today so people might continue to know of his love?

God really took two chances on humankind. The first chance he took was in our creation. The second chance was in our redemption. And he did both without any assurance about how we would respond. First, he created us free, free to choose whether we would live in cooperation with him or in rebellion against him. This is and always has been a real and honest choice. As persons we are not like robots, programmed to respond in a predetermined way. We have a genuine choice. What a chance he took! Also, God took a chance on love by sending Jesus into the world. He became like us, so that we might become like him. In every way he became human, and he was subject to all of the difficulties of human existence. Through Jesus God proves his love to us in that while we were yet sinners, Christ died for us—taking a chance on love.

Now, from this two-pronged fact of amazing grace, I would like to make two points, both in the form of questions and both of which have everything to do with your salvation and with mine. This is the first question: Can anyone remain indifferent to a love that runs so deep and risks so much? Can you say no to the kind of love that is made evident in the life and death of Jesus? There is an anonymous verse we sometimes set to music and sing that says it better than anything else I know. And if this verse sounds too extravagant, it is because the extravagance is indicative of the inexplicable nature of God's love for humankind.

> Could we with ink the ocean fill,
>   Were the world of parchment made,
> Were every single stick a quill,
>   Were every man a scribe by trade:
> To write the love of God alone
>   Would drain the ocean dry:
> Nor could the scroll contain the whole
>   Though stretched from sky to sky.

This is the kind of love that bids us come—come follow Christ. Can we say no to such love that runs so deep and risks so much?

The second point, like the first, is also a question. If God so believes in the value of human beings, if he so loves and trusts people, should we not go and do likewise? Jesus has so clearly said to us, "Love one another, even as I have loved you." It is easy to allow sentimentalism about everybody in general to take the place of our loving anybody in particular. Do you know some person who, by the standards of the world, is unlovable—some irascible person who is usually avoided by others? Why not take a chance on what some expression of love could do to reach that person in a creative and redemptive way?

In the last scene of Marc Connelly's moving play *The Green Pastures,* the Lord is looking out over the parapets of heaven trying to decide what to do with the sinful people on earth. Gabriel, putting his trumpet to his lips to keep the feel of it, asks, "Lawd, is de time come for me to blow?" Without breaking his gaze, God replies, "Not yet, Gabriel." The Lord has decided not to *send* anyone to save his people; this time he has decided to go himself.[1]

God was in Christ, reconciling the world to himself. God proves his love for us in that while we were yet sinners Christ died for us. The Bible verse we learned from John 3:16 is marvelously true: "God so loved the world that he gave his only Son, that whoever believes in him should not perish but have eternal life."

> Joy to the world! the Lord has come:
> Let earth receive her King:

---

[1] Marc Connelly, *The Green Pastures: A Fable* (New York: Holt, Rinehart and Winston, 1967).

TIGERS IN THE DARK

Let every heart prepare him room,
And heaven and nature sing.

Taking a chance on love is our main business—and it is by this risky business that we are saved. God took a chance on love—will you?

THOMAS LANE BUTTS

Thomas Lane Butts was born and reared in Conecuh County, Alabama. Educated in Alabama's public schools, he is a graduate of Pensacola Junior College and Troy University. After receiving graduate degrees in theology from Emory University and in pastoral psychology from Northwestern University, he was awarded a Doctor of Divinity degree from Huntingdon College.

He has served United Methodist churches in Alabama and West Florida for more than 40 years and served four years as a district superintendent in the United Methodist Church. He is currently pastor of the First United Methodist Church in Monroeville, Alabama. He has represented the church at jurisdictional conferences and has served on the boards of many church institutions. He has written for numerous periodicals and has taught religion, psychology and ethics in several colleges. He once received the "School Bell Award" in Florida for outstanding service in the field of education.

Dr. Butts was selected as the preacher for the United Methodist series of the Protestant Radio Hour for 1978. This series of fifteen broadcasts was aired on a nationwide network of radio stations. His book, *Tigers in the Dark*, was originally published by Abingdon Press in 1978.

Dr. Butts is in frequent demand as a speaker on college and university campuses and as an after-dinner speaker. He preaches in churches throughout the country and has been summer guest minister at Christ Church in New York for the past seven years.

He is married to Hilda A. Tidwell and has two grown children, Lane and Rebecca.